The Other Boy

An Intensely Emotional Voyage

M. STEPHENS HALL

Copyright © A Java Press, LLC Publication, 2021

ISBN: 978-1-7366388-0-4

This is a work of creative nonfiction; memoir; All events described herein happened to the best of the author's memory including dialogue and location. Some names and identifying details of people described in this book have been altered to protect their privacy. Any offenses are unintentional.

First printing edition 2021

For my wife Cassie, the only other person in the world who felt the daily emotional strain of the debilitating, arduous war we were thrust into together so many moons ago. I'm extremely thankful I got to fight alongside you. This book is a gift—*for you.*

"Hardships often prepare ordinary people for an extraordinary destiny." - C.S. Lewis

CONTENTS

INTRODUCTION

If you're looking for a book that paints a picture of a perfect life and gives you a step-by-step process for how we've gotten to this point in existence with pithy messages like, "We are so blessed," or conversely defeatist messages like, "We are being punished," then you're reading the wrong book. This book gives a personal account of a roller coaster journey from the viewpoint of a sensitive, intuitive father and husband who feels deeply, not only for his family but for all of humanity. This book tells the story of a real struggle by a real person. It shows how emotionally, mentally, physically, and spiritually draining life's battles can be and how my family and I have survived them.

Life, in and of itself, is a blessing. I believe there is no life without suffering, and I'm of the opinion that blessings can be found in the resulting struggles of that suffering. Blessings are almost always found in discomfort. It doesn't mean I haven't complained at times. It doesn't mean I haven't wished things were easier. It doesn't mean I haven't desired comfort or sought rest at times. Like anyone else, I have longed for all of these things. I'm only human, after all.

I also believe pain is relative. Women typically have a higher physical pain tolerance than men. Of course they do, they are designed to birth babies. Can you imagine a man birthing a baby? Based on my typology studies, I believe personality type can also play a role in a person's pain tolerance. There are a hundred other reasons people handle pain differently, and not just physical pain, but emotional pain as well.

I may seem to handle certain things as if I'm some sort of cold robot, but the truth is, whether I've been conditioned in such a way or built a specific way, or both, there are particular types of intense pain that I am able to carry in my daily walk. It doesn't mean the pain doesn't hurt, it just means that I can carry it and continue to function in my life on a daily basis. Some may see that as a blessing. Others may see it as a curse. I see it as just life.

Pain is often a driver for fear. We're afraid of pain, but perhaps what we're even more afraid of is shock, the shock of jumping into that cold pool. Just the thought of hitting that ice-cold water makes me squirm a bit. Knowing I'll experience a period of paralysis as every nerve in my body fires and then sleeps, even if only for a few seconds, is enough to make me second guess taking that plunge. What we often find, however, is that once we're in the pool, we take a few deep, uncomfortable breaths, then we're fine. We may remain in discomfort for a short time, or even the entire time we're in the pool, but we're fine. We're breathing, we're thinking, and we're alive. We're functioning. We are fine!

I believe in God, the Christian God to be more specific. I give Him glory and I have gratitude for everything in my life, good or bad, but the purpose of this book is to share my emotions, my struggles, and to paint a vivid picture of an arduous journey, not to sugar coat life with religious phoniness. I want this book to be spiritual, not religious. I'm not interested in religion. My commission with this book is so much deeper than that. Religion didn't play a role in this journey for me, but spirituality was vital. Besides, I would never dishonor such a strong message of miracles and hope through processed evangelism.

I hope you'll read this book regardless of your religious or spiritual beliefs. If there's one area I've grown in tremendously over the past twelve years, it's in respect for the beliefs of others. It's not an attitude of, "Oh you believe something different? Well, I'll love you anyway, even though you're wrong." That's not respect. Respect is, "We're all in this together. We're all on a spinning rock that is rotating around a slowly exploding star whose radioactive plasma would melt us if not for invisible energy fields which protect us from that star's savagery." To make this existence even more amazing, we're one of a million other galaxies, so if you believe something different than I do, it's completely fine with me because we're both just searching for answers while we struggle together.

Some may scoff at this attitude, but it's what I believe and it's how I process. So, please know that if I mention God or my belief in God in this book, I don't mean to push anything onto you in any way, it's just me revealing more of myself to you. My hope is that you gain a new perspective, and if not, then at the very least join in a mutual respect with me for the beliefs of others as we spin around on this giant rock together. Besides, Christians aren't the only ones who get cancer. Cancer doesn't choose people by what religion or spirituality they practice, and survivors of cancer aren't chosen because they believe one thing over another. I've often pondered how many religious people think it does though. Sadly, I've been around enough judgmental, brusque, short-sighted religious people to know that number is higher than it should be.

Another purpose of this book is to offer hope to anyone who feels like they can't find any in life's tumultuous storms, and to show them the treasure which the key of hope unlocks—gratitude. I want everyone who has experienced the same fear and helplessness we have to benefit from our story in some way.

This book is written from my personal experience. Even though my wife, Cassie, and I experience most of life together, we are different. We have contrasting but compatible personalities and unique backgrounds, we handle emotions in various ways, and we process life from our own perspectives. Although I know her well, I cannot speak to anything but my perception of how she felt during the events covered in this book.

I don't like to use the word "I" because it feels selfish. At work, I try to always use the word "we." When I speak of my family's experiences, I use the word "we." In this book, however, I will be using the word "I" quite a bit because I want this book to be unique to my experiences as a father in this journey. Even though it feels frightfully uncomfortable, I think I need to take this approach to truly paint my picture and hopefully offer inspiration, especially for fathers who were, will be, or are currently on a similar journey, and have felt the weight of the world on their shoulders, as I have.

I carry an incredible amount of gratitude with me daily. It weighs my heart down like a bag of precious gems. I'm grateful for the opportunity to shine as brightly as I possibly can for a God who came to me and told me this adventure would not be easy, that there would be suffering, but that I could also find peace in it.

I've felt that peace through each storm we've faced.

THE GATHERING

*A*bsent of trepidation and worry, I stood on a small wooden stage before a large crowd. As someone who carries a lot of nervous energy and never seems to get the breathing quite right, I was perversely calm. To be honest, I'm not sure I was breathing at all. Even gravity was just—inexplicably different. It was weaker, lighter, and less of a strain. Perhaps I was on Mars. Time moved more slowly than normal as I methodically addressed friends, family, and complete strangers. They were hanging on my every word as I offered up a eulogy that would make soldiers weep. All the anger, fear, and regret was gone. I felt numb. The blood, tears, and mistakes were all left out on the battlefield to wither away, as the coming years would surely cover them with little to no acknowledgement of the significance they represented. Absolutely no apologies would be granted. My second born son, Xavian, was gone and he wouldn't be walking back through *the door.*

The gathering, since I don't like the term funeral, or actual funerals for that matter, took place in a theater of sorts. This large, open room had a classic Roman empire architectural feel to it, square in shape, consisting almost exclusively of tuff and brick-faced concrete. It felt rigid as kinetic energy accelerated, with only human flesh to slow its disorder. Warm sun rays beamed in gloriously and peacefully through the back of the theater, creating a calm and relaxing mood as our yellow dwarf star, weary from the long summer day, began to tuck himself into bed just beyond the horizon, allowing dusk to provide the respite we so desperately anticipated.

Weightless dust particles danced leisurely in conspicuous beams of light. The temperature was so perfect that it could not be felt. It was as if it didn't exist and couldn't be elucidated. A slight breeze occasionally made its way through the crowd, offering moments of emotional restoration, cooling warm tears as they clung to cheeks as if they, too, wanted to hear what I had to say.

The contrast and disparity of the faces in the crowd paid tribute to the values of inclusion and acceptance which my wife Cassie and I had instilled in our children and drew hard, clear boundaries around. The people sat quietly and gazed upon me with love, honor, sympathy, and even anticipation in their eyes. The mixture of faces reminded me of Autumns past, where all the warm colored leaves combined to paint their own picture in the skyline.

That long-lost compadre, who had come out of the woodwork after hearing through the grapevine that the second born child of his old running mate had passed, looked on apprehensively. That person who I'd parted ways with in conflict years prior sat humbly, swatting at regrets as they swarmed their heart like horse flies. Family members looked on pensively, wishing they could have done more, wanting to be tightly wedged into a process that was only big enough for five, but proudly knowing they did all they could. Friends from various phases of our lives sat adjacent to one another as perfect strangers who didn't realize the impact they had made on us. Xavian's healthcare professionals, who had loved him and cared wholeheartedly about us like we were their family, were reminded of the powerful purpose of their work. The calluses on their hearts, created by the ascension of many beautiful souls, made them strong. Many of the faces in the crowd were unfamiliar. Friends who I'd never met in person joined in the celebration of my son.

My message to everyone was one of love and gratitude, and my words sought to connect with their emotions. I continued my attempt to honor my son by painting a beautiful picture of his courage in a world where his needs were, for the most part, an afterthought, and where people were largely annoyed with his extroverted expression, or couldn't accept that we didn't follow their traditions or live our lives according to their standards.

My son deserved to be honored, even though I felt completely inadequate in doing so. The song "Say Hello to Heaven," which was written and performed by my favorite artist—the late, great Chris Cornell—with members of Pearl Jam as part of the supergroup Temple of the Dog, played softly in the background of my mind. The music spoke to me so deeply and powerfully and served as a portal to a safer place when I needed it the most. An overwhelming desire for all who had gathered to see past my pain and discomfort, and directly into the heart of the trials our family faced daily, drove me. My message came through in a heartfelt, transparent style, delivering truth and offering understanding for all the sacrifices our family made.

The apprehensive, somber emotions of every person gathered drew into me like a vacuum, yet I remained expressionless and emotionless. I literally felt nothing. I had already experienced all the feelings I ever needed. The gathering was for them, not me, and it was for my son. The wind began to pick up as the yellow sun turned orange. The sky glowed softly with velvety hues of purple and pink as the sun quickly set on the horizon. The faces in the crowd turned from apprehension to solace and everyone began stirring.

Hugs were exchanged as humbled hearts exited, but I hugged no one. I had nothing left to give, not even a hug. So, I vanished— out of sight and memory. It marked the end of a journey, a journey to which Cassie and I had given everything we had, where we were defeated and revived a million times over, and where empty tanks held us hostage in the place we remained. My son was gone and he wouldn't be walking back through that door. The fight was over. A new chapter would begin.

TEAR FACTORY

There are said to be three types of tears: psychic tears, which contain certain proteins and hormones absent in other types of tears, are produced as a result of extreme emotions; basal tears, which are released during blinking, help keep the cornea nourished, lubricated, and protected; and reflex tears, which are produced in response to external stimuli, like foreign bodies, or internal stimuli, like stress. In an article published in 2014 by Lorna Collier, through the American Psychological Association, it was reported that findings from a 1980s study by biochemist William H. Frey, PhD, showed that women cry about 5.3 times per month. Men, on the other hand, only cry about 1.3 times per month. Of course, there's the age-old debate which pits testosterone against the hormone prolactin. More specifically, the theory is testosterone, typically higher in men, inhibits crying while prolactin, typically higher in women, promotes crying. Of course, crying isn't all about nature, as pressure from things like social expectations, cultural norms, and freedom of expression logically affect how much a person cries.

Crying has many benefits as well. On a surface level, Lysozyme, a special enzyme found in tears, helps protect our eyes from harmful bacteria which try to invade our body. When we cry, our parasympathetic nervous system (PNS) activates a process that stimulates tears. Research has shown this results in self-soothing. Less directly, but just as important, tears invite hugs, which lead to the release of Oxytocin, also known as the "cuddle hormone," in our bodies. The release of Oxytocin is known to reduce stress, relieve pain, and help induce sleep.

I've gone years at a time without crying, on multiple occasions. As astonishing as such a feat is, it's equally annoying and extremely painful. I told no one about my inability to cry as I developed other ways to release my emotions—for example, exercise—but nothing compared to the cathartic release I experienced from crying. Apparently, the frustration of not being able to cry actually led to such increasingly elevated emotions that those psychic tears finally flowed freely—three years later.

I remember times during that three-year period where I wanted to cry so badly. I wanted to weep, but the tears didn't come.

Any attempt to ignite the type of emotion that could produce tears resulted only in anger or frustration. There was not so much as a convulsion in my abdomen or lump in my throat. None of the pre-cry processes ever happened, and thus crying never happened. The emotion was simply trapped inside me, desperately looking for a way out, as it failed to find an exit. Talking didn't help. Exercise sometimes helped temporarily, but it didn't bring tears. There was no relief, only discomfort. I could have used Bob, the huggable character from the movie *Fight Club*. Bob had these—well, just watch the movie and you'll see what I'm referring to. Just as a drought kills anything green that grows, it felt as if my drought (of tears) was killing me.

Other times in my life, the tears came, and came—and came. I remember sitting in a small downtown coffee shop, working, hiding my face from everyone else there. They didn't need to see the tears streaming down my face, for no apparent reason to them. It was no concern of theirs. The gal behind the counter was concerned, however. I think she could sense something was amiss. I kept waiting for her to walk over to me as she concernedly peered in my direction every few minutes. I got it together though. A few trips to the restroom did the trick. Of course, my puffy, red eyes couldn't be hidden. Cold water helped, but the eyes didn't lie. The eyes never lie. They told stories of strain and distress.

The next day—same thing, different place. The following day—same thing. It's often difficult to discern matters of emotion. For me, I tend to feel others' emotions strongly, even absorb their emotions, so sometimes I'm crying the tears of others instead of my own. Like Peter Petrelli, the main character in the 2006 TV series *Heroes*, experienced with his ability to absorb others' powers, it can be a bit overwhelming to absorb so much from another person. It is interesting that Peter Petrelli is portrayed by Milo Ventimiglia, who also portrayed a character named Jack Pearson in the 2016 TV series *This is Us*, a show that quite frankly makes everyone cry. It's a tangled web of emotion and we are all trapped in it.

Of course, there's the fascinating question of whether "real men" cry. I can settle this right now. Real men cry. Yes, real men cry. In fact, I will add that the more real the man, the more in touch with his emotions he is. That means he is empathetic when his lady cries 5.3 times per month. He gets it and he might even cry with her. Crying can be extremely therapeutic, especially for men who were previously taught crying is a sign of weakness.

On a lighter note, there are also the faces people make when they cry. There's the "cry face." Each of us has an "ugly cry face." I'm more of a shaking type of crier. I don't really do the wrinkled jowl like many people do, but I do shake—quite violently I might add. People who can't see my face when I'm crying, due to the fact that my hands are usually covering it, may even mistake my crying for laughing. Usually, after crying I squint my eyes for a while, perhaps because they are puffy and red. If I ever cry, then glare at you, just know that I'm not mad at you. I just got done crying and I can't stop squinting. We're all good.

By 2005, eight years into a career in software development, I was stressed and frustrated professionally. I couldn't see a job-related future that appealed to me and I couldn't express my emotions in a well-organized manner, but most importantly, I couldn't cry. I was considering leaving the field of software development altogether. I was fairly newlywed and it most definitely affected my marriage in a negative way. It was a very unhappy time in my life when I should have been the happiest person on the planet. In 2007, as I continued to grapple with uncertainty, a good friend and manager at work named Jeff, perhaps sensing my struggles, offered me the following nugget of wisdom:

"Nothing is permanent."

That's all he needed to say, and he knew it. His message was received loud and clear—things change and nothing stays the same. I didn't need to get too down in the dumps over something that may look completely different in a matter of years, months, or even weeks. Over the years, I've shared this wisdom with many people who have come to me for help while sad or in despair over their situation or circumstances at that time. My slightly less concise twist on this proverb goes like this:

"You never know what is waiting for you right around the corner. Expect things that are out of your control to change, and expect everything to be out of your control."

Little did I know at that point in time, as I struggled with who I was and what I was doing with my life, that Jeff's wise words and my own proverb would speak with such a loud voice in my life. Equally as profound, I had no idea that my tears and my emotions, which had dried up like a shallow stream during a drought, would be given ample opportunity to flow—very soon.

THE MOVE

I used to think when something good happened in my life, maybe through someone else's actions or some gained enlightenment, that it was always *directly* divine, purposed, or required. I no longer believe that. While I do still believe we each have a distinct purpose, I also believe life is full of branching paths, and each path takes us to unique destinations. Each path can also take us to places we could have gotten to from other paths. These paths don't all directly serve a higher purpose, but they most likely indirectly do. I don't lose mental and emotional energy or feel inferior to people who would have me believe otherwise. I just look for the purpose in things.

The funny thing about purpose is it isn't sitting in the middle of the path just waiting for someone to walk by and pick it up. It's almost always buried, and finding it often involves two things—discomfort and perspective. Seldom is anything great in life found while we're comfortable. Whether it be mental, emotional, or physical pain, a dose of suffering always gets us closer to that next significant discovery.

Then there's the matter of perspective. Rarely, if ever, have I found something magically concealed within me without searching for it from various perspectives. That painstaking task of admitting we might not have the best view of something should catapult us up and off the couch to which our butts are stuck and toward something fresh and new. Conversely, anytime I look at something the same way repeatedly, something remarkable happens—it *never* changes.

As I've learned so much about myself over the past few years, what has been the most special to me, and maybe the most useful, is how well I'm able to shift perspectives. In basic terms, it means I'm able to naturally and consciously switch from one viewpoint to another. A lot of people claim they can do this, but few actually can, at least not as organically and effortlessly as what I'm referring to. Switching perspectives and knowing I'm wired to do so has helped me so much in recent years.

Living in fear of mundanity for so long took me to terrible, dark places and I'm thankful to have escaped that mental pitfall. I think a lot about how some people live in one place their entire lives while others move to new places often. One downside to staying in one place for an entire lifetime is that a person misses out on new adventures. One downside to moving to new places often is that a person leaves behind relationships which can no longer grow the way they could before they moved away. Both have their positive and negative traits.

I know now that I'm more naturally the person who doesn't stay in one place for too long. Ever since I left Mississippi, my life has been immensely better. I was stuck in one perspective, unable to see the others which awaited me. These new perspectives helped me learn so much about myself; most ironically, I need to move around more so that I don't become stagnant due to a lack of perspective-shifting.

After leaving a place I had lived for the first thirty-one years of my life, the unlocking of this natural ability served me well as, unbeknownst to me at the time, life would soon intensify. During the Winter of 2007, while Cassie, our first-born son Dante, and I were living in Mississippi, we were offered a relocation package by my company and told they'd fund two trips to our new city, Birmingham, Alabama, to help us search for a new home. I recall the two trips we took to this new city.

As we embarked on our first trip to Birmingham, we were filled with excitement. This adventure, which featured a pregnant

Cassie, an infant Dante, and yours truly, was just what the doctor ordered. Our spirits were high and so was the southern heat on an unseasonably warm November day. Within an hour and a half though, our excitement dulled as the stretch of interstate between Meridian, Mississippi, and Tuscaloosa, Alabama, was about as entertaining as watching grass grow. When we approached Tuscaloosa, a college town that sits an hour south of Birmingham, our eager spirits began to dance again at the thought of our new city's foothills not far off.

Then my truck started to sputter. It became clear we weren't going to make it much further, and we had a decision to make—fight through it and push forward on to Birmingham or exit the interstate and have my truck inspected. We chose the latter—and we chose right. My ailing Dodge Ram truck, only five years of age at the time, glided into bay two of the nearest auto repair shop and promptly died. If we had been forced to stop for any reason, we most assuredly would have been *pushing* the hobbled Ram into bay two.

The mechanic, sitting around with greasy hands and a peanut butter sandwich, didn't seem bothered by the taste of motor oil. He did seem confused by a Ram truck, making about as much noise as an electric car, coasting into his bay. After a brief discussion with "The Boss," a middle-aged man with a scruffy beard, basketball gut, and a smell like molasses mixed with oil and coffee, we parked ourselves in a cramped waiting area. There were no other people there. It was so small.

I could feel my shoes roll over the dirt as we walked through. Grime stuck to my hands like glue as I sat down. The air quality couldn't have been good in that place. I wondered if it was safe for an infant. An hour crawled by, but we had received no word on the Ram. There were moments when the hands of the analog clock didn't seem to move as it mocked us from its abnormally high mounting place upon the wall.

As rank as the auto repair shop smelled, it was just as cramped. In such a small space, there weren't enough chairs for every customer to sit down, so people were forced to stand, hovering over those who were seated. Another hour went by, but there was no word. I worried we had made a huge mistake by stopping at that particular place. Another hour, and finally word came from the repair bay—a computer part needed to be replaced. The Boss offered up plenty of details, along with the total repair cost, neither of which was the worst-case scenario. After four long, uneasy hours of sitting in boredom and inconvenience in that grimy waiting area, Dante's patience was plummeting while pregnant Cassie's back pain skyrocketed. Thankfully, only moments later I was able to make my way through the bamboo forest of standing customers, pay The Boss, and get us on our way to Birmingham.

The rest of the trip was uneventful, although we felt rather apprehensive each step of the way, as we visited apartment complex after apartment complex. They all felt the same–congested and boring—and we left Birmingham undecided on a new home. Ultimately, the truck problems, coupled with our inability to find a new home, left me feeling like my alarm clock of intuition had sounded, but I hit the snooze button and tried to fall back asleep amidst the uneasiness.

Our second trip, in the spring of 2008, began in a monsoon in Mississippi. The excitement we'd felt when we departed for our first trip had morphed into nervousness and anxiety on the outset of the second journey. That same stretch of interstate between Meridian and Tuscaloosa wasn't as boring the second time around, as we braved the raging monsoon like pirates on the Caribbean Sea. We blasted through Tuscaloosa without breaking down. Cassie and I beamed with ebullience on our faces, like, "T-town can't hold us down this time."

When we reached Birmingham, however, we ran into more vehicle trouble. Our celebration was a bit premature. It looked like the Ram may not have been cut out for four-hour trips. We were forced to pull over where we were—on the side of the interstate. After being marooned there with an infant during the end-of-day rush hour traffic, we found ourselves riding in the front seat of a wrecker to another auto repair shop.

This time, the Dodge would not be coasting quietly into a mechanic's bay. Instead, he'd be pulled around town by Tow Mater's long-lost cousin. Luckily, the aromatic cigar being French kissed by the wrecker driver reigned supreme over the other pungent odors attacking us from every direction in the cab. Once we arrived at the auto repair shop, four miles away in a very nice part of town, we were greeted by a balding gentleman wearing a grey jumpsuit and sporting a smile like he lived in Mayberry, North Carolina. This mechanic, a much cleaner, better smelling, more welcoming fella than The Boss in Tuscaloosa, quickly determined that my truck needed a new radiator, so it got one—in record speed. It was like this real-life Goober Pyle had it waiting for us behind the desk in his shop.

Even though the trip was cut short, we somehow managed to find a place to live. We also found a very good mechanic. I knew the vehicle trouble represented something, but I couldn't yet put my finger on exactly what.

"Are these truck problems just random bumps in the road, or is this some sort of metaphorical glance into the future?" I racked my brain for answers. "Something doesn't feel right."

Other questions swiftly moved in and out of my mind like

a bullet train, but I kept coming back to the question of whether or not we should move. A case for staying in Mississippi was quickly expanding. I wanted to move. I didn't want to stay there. I'd wanted to leave for so long. Intuition was bringing information, but I wasn't able to decipher it. It was a very concerning time for me.

"Surely a storm is coming," I reasoned with myself. "How can I go through with this when every time we go there something bad happens?"

Foresight is never without a sense of intuition.

I believe things happen for a reason, whether in a direct or indirect way. That branching paths theory I mentioned earlier most likely comes into play in every situation in our lives, and I believe it works in conjunction with things happening for a reason, not against it. Regardless of paths or reason, back then all I knew was the pressure was rising and intuition was pulsating like the chest of an angry dog.

INTUITION, MEET REALITY

Less than two months after we moved to Birmingham, my grandmother passed away at the age of seventy-one. She had always acted much younger than her age and had told me on many occasions that she planned to live well into her hundreds. I believed her; I had no reason not to. But it was her time to go, and she joined my grandfather, who had passed almost exactly nine years earlier.

What followed was a sad time for our family, but also a time of celebration. Almost four months after losing my grandmother, I gained something else precious, my second son, Xavian. He was born on November 24, 2008, three days before Thanksgiving, in Birmingham, Alabama. Unlike his brother, who came into the world with very short, blonde hair, Xavian came into the world with a head full of thick, dark hair.

On a cold, gray and cloudy day in February of 2009, I walked into our small apartment unit after a long day of work. The new position I'd taken when we moved was full of mounting pressure and extra responsibilities, and no one appeared to possess the ability to pull all the loose company ends together except me. Still, it seemed like any other day. My one-year-old son, Dante, was playing with his toys on the living room floor. Errant sun rays, which snuck through the westward-facing porch door, cast shadows of toy trucks, building blocks, and an iPod. Dante was always such a well-behaved child who could play independently just as well as he could with other kids.

From the living room, I could hear the unmistakable sound of baby nursing-grunts. Cassie was in our bedroom feeding Xavian, who experienced a lot of colic as a baby. A typical feeding resulted in screaming, an arched back, and clenched fists. As I started down the hallway toward our bedroom, a strange feeling came over me. It wasn't cold chills. It wasn't anxiety. It was just…weird and inexplicable. I stopped, took an awkward step to the side, almost fainting, leaned against the hallway wall, and gazed into the darkness at the end of the hallway while that strange feeling swept all the way from my head down to my toes.

Something was coming; not physically, not now, but it was coming, and soon. I could feel it. I couldn't explain it, but I most certainly felt it. And, yes, I was scared. As was the case when my truck broke down during our exploratory visits to Birmingham the previous year, I couldn't decipher this new information, but it was prodding me from all directions, begging me to respond.

Intuition can be tricky. It's more feel or *gut* than it is logic. It's often difficult to determine the source of those bursts of magical information, because the information gathering occurs subconsciously. I frequently have "ah-ha" moments in my life, like the time I knew a friend would soon be moving. I hadn't seen or been told anything to give me the impression they were moving, but that's what was given to my conscious mind by my subconscious. Surely enough, I found out a month or two later that they had indeed moved, and told no one. In that sense, intuition can often feel magical or fantasy-like, especially for people like me who live more in their minds than they do the world around them. Intuition can also feel scary, but don't mistake that feeling for fear. Fear comes later and is more of a choice.

That cold February day in 2009, intuition brought me something scary and I became afraid, but how could I talk to anyone about a feeling I didn't fully understand? I have a hard enough time generally articulating my feelings in spoken word, much less a massive cloud of information that tells my gut, "Something is coming and it's bad." I didn't want to believe it, so I dismissed it. I didn't want to be scared.

A few days after the paralyzing feeling that something bad was coming, I got the news that a dear friend's father had been diagnosed with cancer and would be starting treatment soon thereafter. I sat in my truck that evening, weeping for my friend and her family. I wanted to believe that this was the storm that was headed our way, but again, intuition spoke to me and said it wasn't. It didn't leave me empty-handed, though. After some meditation and prayer, I came away from this news feeling like this was part of my original intimation, and the message was, "Prepare yourself. There's more."

Less than two weeks later, while I was at work, I got a call from Cassie to come home. She said Xavian, then two-and-a-half-months old, wasn't doing well. She was very concerned. It was already late in the work day, so I left and headed home.

I felt like something was terribly wrong. When I arrived home, Cassie told me that Xavian had been screaming as if he was in pain for most of the day, except for the times when he was sleeping. He had also fallen asleep repeatedly throughout the day, which was completely abnormal. Cassie was already exhausted, and worry was written all over her face. I quickly jumped into the deep end of distress.

I didn't want to admit that this was the bad thing my intuition had brought to me just a few weeks earlier, but in hindsight, I'm certain it was. I was more scared than I'd ever been. My heart raced. My head hurt. It felt like I was on fire. I needed to vomit. I didn't want intuition to meet reality, but it was happening. As parents, Cassie and I had a big decision to make. Since our pediatrician's office was closed for the day, we either had to wait until the next day to have Xavian checked out or we had to take him to the emergency room.

Fear screamed loudly, straight into the eardrum of my heart. I didn't want to admit that something was wrong. I was in denial. I suggested we wait until the following morning, then take him to the pediatrician, but I wasn't married to the idea. Cassie was convinced we should take him to the emergency room as soon as possible, and I most definitely didn't disagree, so that's what we did.

Traffic was heavy. It seemed when we juked left, the other cars did too. When we dashed right, they dashed even quicker. It felt like the Thriller video. The screaming sound of an infant served as a siren. After fighting our way through five o'clock traffic, we arrived at Children's Hospital. That thirteen-mile trek had seemed more like thirty. Absent of anything other than concrete, the Children's Hospital 7th Avenue Parking Deck felt cold and barren. The lights in the deck were on and winter was in the air on a wet, foggy evening.

Looking back, it felt like something you'd see on The Walking Dead. Fortunately, there were no "walkers" in this parking deck, besides us. We were relatively young parents of two kids less than two years old, one of which was less than three months old. We definitely felt like zombies. Once we parked our vehicle, we had to walk a long distance with Xavian in his car seat. Burning bolts of electricity shot through my back sharply as we scampered toward the emergency room, which was located on the far side of the hospital from where we were.

Emergency rooms are depressing places, and the route we had to take through the basement to get to the Children's Hospital Emergency Room was drab at best. Other than the employees who really enjoy their job, nobody wants to be there. It's not a place that you walk into and everyone is smiling and celebrating. Everyone waiting looks so helpless, if not hopeless. The mood is morbid and dreary. The caretakers, who are concerned for their loved ones, react in a variety of ways as they wait in a place where time seems to stand still. Some feel angry and irritated, while others feel defeated and sad. Some even have anxiety attacks.

To add to the irritation brought on by simply sitting in an emergency room waiting area, being sunbathed by fluorescent lighting, each patient must be triaged. This is a process whereby the hospital staff gauge the severity of the patient's condition, which directly affects the priority order for all patients. A patient with a runny nose and low-grade fever is always going to get lower priority than one who has a history of cancer or a partially severed limb, for example. It's logical to me, although being on the lower end of that priority list undoubtedly ignites a fire that consumes logic.

As Cassie and I waited, especially concerned for Xavian, I optimistically hoped we would be in and out quickly, sent home with a prescription, and encouraged to get better soon. Somehow, I knew better. Our hearts pounded in rhythm like a pair of bass drums at a hard rock concert. Air felt heavy and thick as it moved slowly through our chests. Our exhales were pronounced and our eyes told a story of concern and fear, just like every other parent sitting in that waiting room. It created a surreal mood that posed an impossible question, "Is this really happening?" Nightmares are synonymous with fear, and emergency rooms are what nightmares are made of—oh the horror of those fluorescent lights.

It wasn't long before a staff member called out, "Hall." Apparently, since Xavian was so small, we had been given a higher priority. Having your name called after an uneasy wait, for me at least, always yields a mixed bag of emotions. It starts with an elated feeling of disbelief, followed by brief processing of the moment. Next comes the confirmation through eye contact with the clerk.

Once the eyes confirm what the mind suspects, I move. Lastly, I feel empathy for those families who are forced to remain in that fluorescent light oven. Of course, this all happens in only an instant, but the butterflies never cease to swarm.

The next six to eight hours in that emergency room are a blur. I say "six to eight hours" because I honestly do not remember what time we were called back to a room, but I do remember leaving sometime after midnight, perhaps even closer to two or three o'clock the next morning. While Xavian's symptoms continued to alternate between sound asleep and awake screaming, the emergency room staff ran test after test, but found no answers. This seemed like a healthy infant on the surface, but the doctors knew something wasn't right, and they didn't give up searching.

There wasn't much conversation between Cassie and I. We were in a cramped, uncomfortable room in an old hospital. We were scared, exhausted, and freezing cold—the kind of cold where you need to pee every twenty minutes. The doctors made me nervous because they had no answers. "Aren't they supposed to figure these things out fairly easily?" I pondered. Fatigue turned into aching. My heart skipped beat after beat. Hunger, headache, and nausea eventually overcame my ability to think straight. I still wanted to believe that whatever my intuition had given me was nothing, but I was too exhausted to even consider the possibilities at that point. I just wanted answers and for my son to be alright.

At some point, the doctors decided to move Xavian from the emergency room to a unit in the hospital known as "Special Care Unit," which is a step-down critical care unit that takes care of children of all ages and diagnoses. In this special care unit, Xavian would receive focused attention by means of direct monitoring. Families were encouraged to stay at the hospital while their patient was in the special care unit. Knowing how weary we were though, our medical staff suggested we go home and sleep while Xavian was kept under close observation, so we staggered back to the parking deck, cold and scared, then made the thirteen-mile trek home. If we weren't zombies when we arrived those many hours earlier, we most certainly were when we departed.

The next morning, we were awoken by the sound of Cassie's phone ringing. It was someone from Children's Hospital. They informed Cassie they had "found something" and asked that we return to the hospital as soon as we could. Panic and nausea set in instantly, getting me moving in spite of not feeling rested. Cassie and I didn't talk much on our drive to the hospital, but quite honestly, what was there to say? I was just trying to make sense of it all. Decrypting this bad dream that I couldn't seem to wake from felt impossible. Still hungry, drained, and scared, we dressed ourselves and left for the hospital.

When we arrived, the walk from the parking deck to the Special Care Unit felt more like a trek across Africa with a hundred pounds of apprehension strapped to our backs. At the unit, we were escorted to a waiting area of sorts. Adjacent to this waiting area was an inconspicuous door that led into a small, rectangular-shaped room with soft lighting, a couch, a few chairs, and an overall relaxing aesthetic.

"Why are they trying to comfort us?" I thought to myself as the remaining puzzle pieces began falling into place.

It was in this room that we were met by a counselor and a surgeon. The counselor was a very kind African-American lady, slightly heavy on the weight, but very heavy on the warmth. She had short dark hair and appeared genuinely concerned. The surgeon was tall with grey hair, although it might be better described as white or silver. He was very matter-of-fact and as cool as the other side of the pillow.

"A surgeon and a counselor?" I thought in horror, becoming increasingly perplexed. "This is not good."

I'm sure they all noticed the crinkling of my forehead, the dubious stare beaming from my eyes, and the lack of blinking. I also may have stopped breathing at some point. This was the moment I knew the airplane was about to drop out of the sky. I hoped a captain's voice would blast through the PA system with some sort of reassurance, but it never happened. I waited for the oxygen masks to drop out of the ceiling, but they never came. This airplane was crashing, and there was absolutely nothing I could do about it. I was helpless and exposed.

Time slowed to a crawl as we took our places in the small room. We sat on the couch facing the door, with Cassie to my left. The counselor and the surgeon each sat in a chair, with the counselor to our left and the surgeon straight across from us. The soft, warm mood lighting offered a relaxing atmosphere, but the reality of the situation served up a platter of anxiety and tension that would have required something much sharper than a butter knife to cut through. Time always moves so slowly when you don't want it to.

As the surgeon explained the situation to Cassie and me, tears began to seep from our eyes. Our son was being prepped for an emergency, life-threatening surgery. There was a large mass in his head, and they gave him a fifty percent chance of surviving the surgery. His best chance at survival was for the mass to be a brain tumor. That didn't sound good. My thoughts immediately trapped me and held me captive in a web of worst-case scenarios. I was just waiting for the spider to glide down and devour me—and it did.

The surgeon seemed confident and eager to get to the operating room to get started. "Do you have any questions for us at this point in time?" he asked impassively.

"I just want this nightmare to end," I cried out and broke down as a trickle of tears turned into a raging river pouring profusely from my eyes. Everyone in the room was in danger of drowning. I can't remember there ever being a time in my life where I wept so uncontrollably in front of other adults. I felt so naked and weak.

All four walls shook. Everyone and everything in the room shook. I was immediately struck with a feeling of lightheadedness. Someone cranked up the volume on the raging noise in my head and muted everything else. My always-confident wife looked rattled, confused, and mystified. She wasn't saying anything. At that moment, I was helpless to provide her support, and I knew it. Of course I didn't have any questions. Reality was shattering into pieces all around me. What was there to ask, and how would I speak if I did have a question?

After a few moments of silence and me trying to compose myself, the doctor left and the counselor led us to the area where we'd be waiting, advising us to prepare ourselves as best as we could. I was prepared for it in the same way one is prepared for a train that is about to obliterate them. I knew it was coming, but there was no way to anticipate the force of the impact, and there was most definitely no stopping it. Intuition had finally met reality, and reality had become a nightmare.

COLD, DARK CUBICLE

My head pounded ruthlessly. It was as if I had just sprinted fifty miles without stopping. I sat in an uncomfortable chair with my palms pressed tightly against my forehead. Whenever I *could* open my eyes, I simply stared at the ground. It was all I could do. My eyesight was blurred at best, and there was persistent ringing in my ears. With each and every heartbeat my head throbbed, my heart ripping apart at the seams. Warmth turned into a pipe dream and my body shook with chills inside a cold, dark cubicle, which stood eerily behind the outpatient surgery registration desk in a gloomy corner at Children's Hospital. Any attempt by vomit to exit my stomach failed repeatedly, leaving me achy and nauseated. All I really wanted was a blanket, but I was so discombobulated that I couldn't even ask for one. My mind held on by a thread, my body shook, and my soul cried out for mercy.

Xavian had been taken back to surgery to go under the knife. Before he was old enough to speak, his skin would be lacerated, his blood would spill out, and our future would be rewritten. In the meantime, we could only wait and pray, in full submission to a higher power. It was out of our control. There was no comfortable private room available at the time of his surgery, so a cubicle was our only option. A cave would have been more comfortable.

Cassie was in the midst of a nasty migraine, which was expected considering the news we had just received. Besides, as a sufferer of chronic migraines, it was nothing new to her. She needed peace and quiet, but neither was available. She was forced to submit to the raw exposure of the blaring world outside of the quiet room she so desperately desired. Her normal retreat to a soft bed in a quiet bedroom simply wasn't an option this time.

Comforting her was impossible when I couldn't even comfort myself, my mind running the surgeon's words in an unending loop. Xavian was having his skull cut open to remove a large mass located in the right hemisphere of his brain. The fifty percent chance of survival given to him by the neurosurgeon was due to the size of the mass, along with his age and the fact that they didn't know if it was a tumor or something more life threatening. The fact that they hoped for a brain tumor painted a profoundly clear picture of the criticality of the situation.

While Cassie's aunt took care of Dante at our home, we needed someone to take care of us at the hospital. This extraordinarily taxing period of hours felt more like days, if not weeks. We needed someone who was well organized, kind and caring, calm under pressure, communicative, and who knew us well. This was where our friend Kym entered the game. We had known Kym for years. She was the wife of the pastor who had presided over our wedding, but more importantly, Kym was our friend and the perfect person to help us through the situation we were in.

She was really good at feeling out situations. She knew when to be assertive and when to take a step back. By some miracle, she was there with us. To this day, I can't think of anyone I'd rather have had on our team. I don't remember many logistical details from that day, and a big part of that is because Kym took care of things while we did everything we could to hold ourselves together. As the day went on, our mothers arrived to provide relief for Kym, who had earned a well-deserved "W" as the starting pitcher, as well as first ballot entry into the Hall of Fame of our hearts for carrying the bulk of the heavy load during a time when our bodies and minds were compromised.

DIAGNOSIS

Xavian survived the surgery, but he wasn't out of the woods yet. As he rested in the recovery room later that day, it was time to discuss what we were dealing with. Still trying to hold ourselves together, we eagerly awaited the news.

"Your son had a massive brain tumor," Xavian's neurosurgeon said as he nodded with both confidence and sympathy. He said "brain tumor" but the written diagnosis read "Malignant Neoplasm of the CNS - NOS, WHO grade IV; right temporoparietal PNET."

PNET is an acronym for primitive neuroectodermal tumor. PNET tumors appear identical under the microscope to medulloblastoma, but occur primarily in the cerebrum. PNET is used by some to refer to tumors such as pineoblastoma, polar spongioblastoma, medulloblastoma, and medulloepithelioma. It is a rare tumor, usually occurring in children and young adults under twenty-five years of age. The overall five-year survival rate is only about 53%. It gets its name because the majority of the cells in the tumor are derived from neuroectoderm, but have not developed and differentiated in the way a normal neuron would, and so the cells appear "primitive." Researchers have not been able to find an identifiable cause or risk factors for PNET. There doesn't appear to be a genetic predisposition, meaning the disease does not seem to run in families.

Malignant Neoplasm of the CNS refers to a central nervous system (CNS) tumor. A CNS tumor begins when healthy cells in the brain or the spinal cord change and grow out of control, forming a mass. A cancerous tumor is malignant, meaning it can grow and spread to other parts of the body. A benign tumor means the tumor can grow but will not spread.

Xavian's tumor was classified as grade IV. In a grade IV tumor, cells in the tumor are actively dividing. In addition, the tumor has blood vessel growth and areas of dead tissue. These tumors can grow and spread quickly—like Xavian's tumor did.

It's much clearer for me today than when we received the diagnosis after surviving that cold, dark cubicle. Back then, I couldn't make heads or tails of this information. It just made my head hurt. I may as well have been trying to read a language I had never seen. "Brain tumor" sounded simple, but "Malignant Neo-plasm of the CNS - NOS, WHO grade IV; right temporoparietal PNET" sounded extremely complex and overwhelming, and possibly grave.

TUBES EVERYWHERE

I f you're a parent, then you remember taking your first child home from the hospital, typically a few days after they were born. It's one of the most frightening things I've ever experienced. It was so frightening that it almost didn't even feel exciting. I remember thinking, "I'm now responsible for this brand new fragile little soul, this innocent, tiny human. I'm so afraid I'm going to make a mistake."

I felt that same fear after Xavian survived the life-threatening surgical procedure that left him with a large horseshoe scar on the right side of his head. The scar started in front of his right ear and circled all the way back to the lower-back-right side of his head. After Xavian's tumor resection surgery, the first thing I *thought* about when I saw him was taking him home and how nervous I would feel in the process. The first thing I *saw* was a tiny infant in a giant hospital PICU bed with tubes coming out of him, each connecting to a different device. There were literally tubes everywhere. It was like something out of The Matrix.

Any thoughts of going home or taking the next step were abruptly replaced with the reality that we were in a war we might actually lose. Overwhelming fear birthed the worst possible outcomes in my mind. Optimism is hard to grab hold of in such situations. Seeing any infant, or any child for that matter, lying in a giant hospital bed with tubes coming out of them cuts like a knife. When it's your own child, it's a serrated knife and cuts you to the core.

Seeing your infant lying there sedated, motionless, and helpless, with random tubes running everywhere, a breathing tube down his throat, and an abnormally large bandage on his head, kills you over and over. It's suffocating. As a parent, you want to take control, reach in, and somehow make it better, but the reality of the situation is the parent is at the mercy of the medical team and you have no other choice but to trust that. We weren't the majority owners; we were just part of the team. In an instant, that hard-to-swallow truth became our reality.

Sometimes knowing your place offers you the best chance for victory. Admitting you aren't in control and don't need to take control in situations where that is exactly the case *greatly* increases your chances of success. Equal to the direness of our situation was the love and warmth we felt from our medical team, namely the PICU nursing staff. While physicians and specialists brought technical knowledge and formulated plans of treatment, and sometimes seemed more like androids than humans, our nursing staff brought love and warmth and a reassurance that they were there to care for us and support us.

Even though our medical team was the highlight of the PICU experience in 2009, the PICU waiting area was *undeniably* the lowlight. To say it left a patient's family with much to be desired would have been the understatement of the year—by a mile. The space was drab. It felt hard and cold and had that same dreadful fluorescent lighting that baked the brains of families who sat in the emergency room waiting area. The floor was dirty and slippery, and the energy of the room increased with each carom against the wall.

Sometimes the fluorescent lights would flicker, sending out cries for help through Morse code. No matter how many human bodies were present, the energy only increased as it moved swiftly around the room. It felt like nothing could slow it down. Not only was the space extremely limited for the potential number of families who might be waiting at a given time, but there was absolutely no privacy.

You may be thinking, "Why do you need privacy in a waiting room?" and you'd be valid in your query. However, this wasn't just a waiting room. It was essentially home for each family who had a child in PICU for the duration of their stay. There were no private rooms for families. Ronald McDonald House and other great organizations like aTeam Ministries in Homewood, AL, offered housing for families who lived long distances from Children's Hospital, but for families like us who lived nearby, temporary housing not only didn't make sense, but we probably didn't qualify for such a thing. Thus, our home became the PICU waiting room for three days.

This insipid space was essentially an ill-colored loft full of families who ate, drank, visited, slept, and grieved together, and who worried for their child, grandchild, niece, nephew, brother, or sister each and every day—exposed and in plain sight of everyone. Surely there was some HIPAA violation hidden therein. I never desired to share such a painful experience with complete strangers. I would have much preferred a private room where I could better collect my thoughts and focus more clearly without feeling like I was intruding on someone else's privacy every time I lifted my head. Life doesn't always give us the options we desire, and it doesn't really respond to criticism either. It just tests us repeatedly until our skin is calloused enough to handle it.

It wasn't too long before friends, co-workers, and family

members began trickling in. Each visitor sparked a different emotion in myself or Cassie. We were deeply appreciative for each and every person who came to check on us. It's always interesting to me, during those times of heightened emotions, how you get a glimpse of the depth at which you are connected to a person. With some visitors, even beloved family members or friends, we exchanged hugs and I was genuinely happy to see them and grateful they had come to visit us. With others, as soon as I saw their faces I broke down into tears, the dam holding back my emotions crumbling under the pressure of our new reality and the profound sentiment they triggered in me, for whatever reason.

THE ROASTER

After three days in PICU, our team of medical professionals felt like Xavian was strong enough to leave the unit, but we weren't going home. Our next stop was the Neurosurgery unit, where patients spend time recovering from neurological-related surgeries and procedures. Unlike our time in PICU, the Neurosurgery floor offered us a private room and a place to actually rest for the first time since we'd rushed Xavian to the hospital only five days earlier. The rooms in the Neurosurgery unit were newly renovated, spacious enough, had a pleasant scent, and came fully equipped with a pull-out couch, which at that time felt like a luxury experience. That was something to get excited about for someone who hadn't stretched their legs out in what felt like months.

Even the lighting there was more relaxing. It meshed well

with the peace and quiet of the unit to create a pleasant environment. Lying down that first time, letting my body go limp with my legs fully extended, felt like heaven. I think I fell asleep instantly. I was on Cloud Nine. Not even the rock-hard cushions and random bumps that felt like metal digging into my spine could deny me that moment of peace. Just being able to yield all control, while Xavian lay peacefully on a gargantuan hospital bed, felt like winning the lottery.

Sleeping offered a different challenge, one that extended far beyond dealing with random metal bumps digging into my back. By that time, Xavian had shed many of the tubes he'd been connected to in PICU, but he still had plenty of tubes and lines connected to his body. It continued to ignite stress in me. One line connected Xavian to a pulse oximeter, which is a device that measures the proportion of oxygenated hemoglobin in the blood in pulsating vessels, especially the capillaries of the finger or ear.

The pulse oximeter Xavian was connected to during his time in the Neurosurgery unit featured a glaring light connected to his big toe. Surely this light had been harvested from Rudolph's nose, as it shone as brightly as a Christmas light. Of course, you'd usually just turn off that sort of light at night, but that was not an option for us. That particular glowing red light demanded my attention. It shouted for me to wake up, to not sleep, and to remain in misery. I felt like Cosmo Kramer, and subsequently Jerry Seinfeld, in the Seinfeld episode, "The Chicken Roaster," where the giant neon signs attached to the Kenny Rogers Roasters restaurant across the street from Kramer and Jerry's apartment complex shone so brightly that they were unable to sleep.

The glowing red light wasn't my only enemy through those long, cold, semi-comfy nights. Whenever the pulse oximeter level would measure too low, Hell's Bells would sound out. I would be awoken from a deep sleep with a prehistoric pterodactyl in our room, ready to strike, warning me of impending doom. I couldn't get far enough away from it or cover my ears well enough to mute it, and I didn't dare turn it off. After all, I had no idea how important the machine was. For all I knew, it could have been my son's lifeline. That's just how novice I was on our new journey. There was no escaping it. That discordant, shrieking alarm would haunt me for the duration of our visit in the Neurosurgery Unit.

Over the remainder of our time there, we received a lot of support from family and friends. I remember my co-workers visiting and bringing us a large jar of quarters so we could get drinks and snacks from the vending machines. I had only known most of them for a few months, so the fact that they joined together and supported us in that way meant a great deal to me, and I don't think I was ever able to express my gratitude enough. The quarters were great, but their kind gesture alone offered warmth like sun rays on a cool autumn day.

When we first arrived at the Neurosurgery unit, I'd fully expected it to become our home for the next week or two. I anticipated a detailed training course by a medical professional in caring for a child who had a large horseshoe shaped incision. I naively thought I'd leave the hospital with the utmost confidence in removing, cleaning and rewrapping the bandages which hugged the part of his head above his eyebrows from front to back. I couldn't have been more wrong. Only a few days in, our medical team decided we were in a great spot to be discharged.

"What? This must be some mistake. They're sending the wrong kid home. I'm not prepared for this," I thought to myself in utter fear as the team huddled around us. It felt like I was slowly shrinking. After the team left our room, I urgently sought out the nurse in charge to inform her of the mistake, but there was no mistake. We were going home.

It was the same feeling I'd experienced after Dante was born less than two years earlier, when they'd sent us home after only two days. Only, this time I wasn't prepared for it and my expectations were met head on by a runaway freight train which had surely gone off the tracks. Was I going crazy or was everyone just a bit too lax on the matter?

Unfortunately, or perhaps fortunately, no mistake had been made. Xavian once again flexed his muscles and showed everyone that he would not be denied life or victory, or even simple progress. His body, though compromised by a brain tumor, brain surgery, lines and tubes, and plenty of needle pokes, was strong and he was healing quickly. We were going home because it was time to go home, and although butterflies set up camp in my stomach and swarmed ferociously, I knew it was time to put on the armor, pick up the sword, and head out to the battlefield for the next phase of the fight. Fear and pressure were at an all-time high, but there were no other options.

NOT EASILY BROKEN

Cassie and I were married in Orange Beach, Alabama, in October of 2005, right on the beach, on the most beautiful day I've ever experienced in my entire life. The weather was so perfect it almost felt imaginary. The only clouds that rolled through the beautiful, deep blue sky that day were a few playful cirrus clouds. There was a slight breeze and the sun seemed less angry than usual for some reason. I remember being nervous but also very relaxed.

Only two months earlier, Hurricane Katrina had ravaged the Louisiana and Mississippi gulf coasts, less than two hours west of our wedding location. Hurricane Katrina was the largest and third strongest hurricane ever recorded to make landfall in the United States, killing almost two thousand people as it barreled through in 2005. By 2014, nine years later, over seven hundred people were still reported as missing as a result of the savage storm. Over fifteen million people were affected in different ways, varying from loss of home to economic suffering. It's estimated that the total economic impact may have exceeded $150 billion, making Hurricane Katrina the costliest hurricane in the history of the United States.

I've often pondered the significance of that storm and how it may have affected the weather, people, and a thousand other things during the time leading up to our wedding. It's hard to imagine that such a picture-perfect day, our wedding day, could have taken place so soon after such a violently devastating storm. If we really think about it though, life works that way so often. Scary, powerful things hit us when we least expect it, sometimes redirecting us onto different paths, other times simply changing what we encounter on the path we're on.

Months before our wedding, we were living in Mississippi, less than an hour away from the direct path of Hurricane Katrina, albeit more than two hours inland. Although we didn't feel hurricane-force winds, we certainly experienced the power of that storm in its diminished state, which was still moderately powerful. As we drove over the dam at the south end of the Ross Barnett Reservoir, a body of water that didn't normally have waves or surf and was usually relatively calm, water crashed violently against the rocks on the dam and somersaulted over our vehicle. The wind shear moved us from side to side. I remember wondering if we should have even been driving over that dam or if the road should have been open at all. As exciting and amazing as it was, it felt very dangerous.

For my adventurous fiancé and I, it was exciting. We weren't about to turn around. We were headed to my aunt's house to hang out during a time when no one had power. The safest route seemed to be the interstate, so that's where we headed. But billboards on the interstate were flying around while debris danced about. We were the running back looking for the right hole to blast through in order to escape the powerful linebackers pressing down upon us. It was anything but safe. The sky was chocolate and vanilla swirl ice cream as the clouds moved round and round. If that was the weakened version of Hurricane Katrina, then the full-strength version of the storm must have been quite a spectacle. It felt apocalyptic. At that point, even the interstate was unsafe, so we exited and thought we'd try going through the suburbs. We obviously didn't think that decision through to conclusion because the suburbs, which were filled with very old, large trees, had been transformed into a maze of downed power lines and large broken tree limbs. We eventually made our way to my aunt's house, but not before our exciting adventure had turned into a genuine feeling of concern for our safety, and if I may be dramatic for a moment, a fight for survival.

I believe that violent storm, one which couldn't stop us from reaching our destination even as angry waves engulfed us, and which annihilated beaches and cities mere miles from the unscathed beach where Cassie and I were wed, in many ways symbolized the strength of a spiritual bond that would not be easily broken.

MOTHERLY INSTINCT

I've been married long enough to give sound advice to young men who are single, engaged to be married, or in a serious relationship. I feel qualified to give advice on the grounds that I have been married for over fifteen years. I've been through physical, mental, and emotional storms with my wife, and through grace, we're still married.

Motherly instinct is like magic, and while personalities and many other factors can certainly influence how a mother processes and works through things, this natural instinct is undeniable. It shined the brightest for me when we arrived home with our first child, Dante, in 2007. I remember thinking to myself, "How did she know to do that?" as my wife went into full-on mother mode. I was completely blown away.

This tiny being was alive and it was all so much bigger than me. I felt thoroughly inadequate, which speaks directly into the heart of the advice I would give to men who might be fathers: You don't have to feel inadequate, because you're not inadequate. Marriage is full of these natural roles, and each marriage is different, thus the roles therein are different. In case you haven't already noticed, I'm not at all traditional. In fact, I've grown to despise tradition because I feel it boxes us in and makes life boring. It most certainly goes against my natural, more future-thinking way of processing. Plus, I believe there is a connection between cognitive processing and energy as it relates to masculinity and femininity.

Tradition can certainly have a loud voice in marriage as it pertains to roles, i.e. "the husband is to do this, while the wife is to do this," but I think it's up to each couple to find what works best for them. Reality tells us that, from a cognitive perspective, there is a preference with regard to masculine and feminine energy. I subscribe to the idea that both individuals should learn one another's natural preference and set expectations based on that information. One size fits all marriages don't seem to last nearly as long as marriages where adjustments are made based on the individuals' needs, or marriages that ebb and flow with constant change—*especially* when under extreme stress.

Going back to the notion of motherly instinct, the second time I stood in amazement of Cassie's motherly instinct was when we brought Xavian home from the hospital after a stint which included a visit to the emergency room, brain surgery, a stay in PICU, and a short stay in the Neurosurgery Unit. Seeing her take command of the situation as she changed his head bandages for the first time, while I played the role of her assistant with her mother by our side for wisdom and support, I didn't feel inadequate at all. Instead, I felt safe and secure, and although I don't remember all the details, I do remember the feeling of a newfound assurance that gave me the confidence to play a certain role to its maximum potential. What my role consisted of was feminine energy in a supporting role of Cassie's more proactive, masculine energy. That particular dynamic would probably give most men hives, but being intentional about it is a key ingredient to a successful marriage.

THE DUNGEON

We were thankful to be back home where we could rest and focus on continued healing. Thankfully, we were blessed with a firstborn who was independent, manageable, and easy going. Don't get me wrong, he was a child and required plenty of parenting, but he was exactly what we needed, when we needed it. He was a breath of fresh air.

We were only able to rest for a few weeks as we adjusted to our new life before being sucked right back into the supercell storm which had moved upon us ever so suddenly. Days of going to the park or meeting Cassie and Dante for lunch were replaced by phone conversations with clinicians, in-person conversations with my company's Human Resources department regarding insurance coverage, and clinic visits to discuss the best plan of action to save my son's life.

In the midst of buying a new home, for which we had placed a contract on just days before we found ourselves in that epic clash against cancer, we began preparations for chemotherapy. Our three-month-old baby who had already been through hell was about to have a non-discriminatory, cell-killing set of drugs known as chemotherapy pumped through his strong, but young infant body. Make no mistake about it, chemotherapy can certainly kill the mutated cells, but it also takes plenty of healthy cells with it, resulting in short-term, mid-term, and long-term side effects, none of which are desirable.

We weren't asked if we wanted to move forward with the chemotherapy treatments, just asked to sign on the dotted line. The decision had already been made. The next phase of this fresh and unexpected battle was about to begin, and whether we were ready for it or not didn't matter. It was happening, and the intensity was about to be dialed up a few notches.

Time passed quickly. I blinked my eyes and a thousand suns seemed to set. Only a few weeks remained in February of 2009 and the time had arrived for us to make the short drive to Children's Hospital of Alabama to begin the chemotherapy treatments. I had heard horror stories about chemotherapy but, surprisingly at thirty-one years of age at the time, I hadn't had any first-hand experience with it, so I honestly didn't know what to expect.

A few days before Xavian's chemotherapy began, I cut my hair, which at the time extended halfway down my back. I feared my long hair would bring germs into an environment which needed to be clean. Whether this was actually a valid concern didn't really matter to me. I was cutting it anyway. I feared infection.

As we took our time packing our bags and making our way to the car, I remember thinking about how surreal it all was. I tried to think of something else, in hopes that the reality we were in would vanish like a dream when you awake, but for each moment that I escaped reality, I was thrust back into it more expediently than when I left. There was no escape.

The drive was short and quiet, and time appeared to stand still. We were moving, but nothing else looked to be moving. Birds stopped in mid-flight, and everything slowed to a crawl. I thought perhaps I was having a mental breakdown or anxiety attack. The sun was shining, but everything around us was dark and eerie, Cassie and I both stuck in contemplative deep thought. My eyes stayed locked on the road, while her eyes gazed out the passenger window. We hardly spoke, but words could serve no dutiful purpose at that time, so why bother? I have no doubt she was as nervous as I was; I didn't need to ask—so I didn't.

Once we arrived at the hospital, the first order of business was registration. In order for Xavian to be admitted, we had to register him. The process was as slow and dull as the cramped room you sat in while signing the papers. The clerks, both expressionless older ladies wearing a tad too much perfume and makeup, sat on the opposite side of a plexiglass divider. It felt like I was in prison and the clerks were visiting me to deliver bad news, of which I could do nothing about. The mood was cold and they didn't seem to want to be there anymore than we did. I understood how they felt.

At one point, I made the mistake of looking up, and there they were—fluorescent lights. Of course there were fluorescent lights. Once registration was complete and we were officially admitted to the hospital, we headed up to the fourth floor where children who received chemotherapy stayed. The feel, the smell, and the whole idea of all these children being in this unit felt very institutional and cold to me, even though I could tell efforts were made to bring more warmth to it. I didn't like the vibe one bit. I wanted it to feel more warm and homey, but in a genuine kind of way.

This unit was more commonly known as Four Tower. The fact that it had a nickname gave me cause to pause. I sensed this unit had a reputation. I pondered whether that was a good thing or a bad thing, but it was too early to tell. Either way, we were about to find out.

When we arrived at Four Tower, we were greeted by some very nice people. My concerns about the coldness of this place thawed a bit—that is, until we got to our room. No one had to tell me this room was called *The Dungeon*. I could see it for myself. Later, I confirmed it. It was tucked away in the back of the unit, around a corner that seemed to double as toy and tricycle storage. I wondered where they kept the dragon.

The hallway outside the room was very dark and it was considerably colder than the rest of the place. The room itself looked old and worn. It was small and not very inviting, but the true horror of it was revealed when I opened the blinds for the first time. The room faced a brick wall with office windows. That's right, there was no view of downtown Birmingham, no view of the beautiful University of Alabama at Birmingham (UAB) campus. There was only brick and a small amount of glass with metal trim. Sometimes there would be a person in that room. I debated whether they took care of the dragon.

Anyhow, there was no direct sunlight. In fact, light struggled to find its way to our room at all. It was difficult to tell what time of day it was. This was the room where our infant son would receive his first cycle of chemotherapy, and there were at least two more cycles scheduled. We feared this dungeon would become our new home. My blood pressure increased. The only question that remained was, "Where is that blasted dragon?"

The first cycle of chemotherapy could best be described as concerning, overwhelming, and slow. My impression of chemotherapy up to that point was mostly based on what I had heard over the years: it makes the patient nauseated and weak, so they vomit constantly; it makes the patient's hair fall out, so they become bald; it can have a lot of side effects, some immediately and some later. The picture painted by my mind was focused on adults, but Xavian was only three months old. I struggled to envision how this chemotherapy would affect such a small human.

Our medical team reviewed with us many of the common side effects that were possible based on Xavian's chemotherapy protocol. It was scary, especially the part about secondary cancers that may develop as a late effect of previous cancer treatments, but that was just one of the potential long-term side effects.

Before I get into the technical side of Xavian's medical treatment, there's the whole issue of timing to consider. As I mentioned, we were in the midst of buying a new home when we entered this battle against childhood cancer. We had already placed a contract on our soon-to-be home and we had found someone to take over the remaining part of our apartment contract. Everything seemed to be falling into place, except for the part where we found out our child had a cancerous brain tumor and would need a resection surgery and at least three cycles of chemotherapy. While we were in the hospital for our first cycle, we would not only need to close on our new home, but we would also need to move all of our belongings to this new home. It simply wasn't going to be possible.

It just so happens, I believe in miracles. And at that time, when we most needed something magical to happen—two things did.

The first thing that happened was our mortgage lender said he would take care of the closing for us. This was an extremely abnormal, but extraordinarily thoughtful action for someone to take, especially since he barely knew us. He even came to the hospital, with papers in hand, so that we wouldn't have to leave our room. There are saints, then there was this man, and I cannot express the amount of gratitude I have for him for helping us in a moment when we were, for all intents and purposes, helpless. I'll add that he gave us a loan for a home when we had a credit score of zero, due to the fact that we hadn't borrowed money in a long time.

The second thing that happened involved our friend Kym, who had helped us so much on the day of Xavian's tumor resection. Spearheaded by Kym and a friend from work, a team of caring people was assembled. This team united and packed up everything we owned from our apartment unit, transported it to our new home, then unloaded and unpacked everything so that we could focus all of our efforts on our family, our son, and the battle at hand. When we arrived home, everything was in its place. It was astounding. It was like a team of angels had been sent down from the heavens to comfort us in strategic and profound ways, and it worked.

Helping someone is often about the person being helped, not the helper necessarily, but these particular angels deserve recognition. Just know that when you help someone, although at times it can feel like your actions didn't make a huge difference, or perhaps seemed mundane and negligible, it's always honorable and purposeful. To the person you helped, it's priceless. As gifts that keep on giving go, it also yields gratitude.

CHEMO AND CHARCOAL

PNETs are highly malignant tumors with rapid tumor progression. Treatment typically includes surgical resection, chemotherapy, and radiotherapy, although in Xavian's case, radiotherapy was not an option due to the fact that he was so young. Despite the current treatment regimens, long-term survival rates still do not exceed 20 to 30%, especially for young children. These survival rates are statistical values though, and provide information on the total cohort of patients with these types of tumors. They don't predict individual outcomes.

A chemotherapy regimen defines the drugs to be used, their dosage, the frequency and duration of treatments, and other considerations. In modern oncology, regimens often include a combination of drugs which work synergistically. Xavian's regimen of chemotherapy agents included Cisplatin, Cyclophosphamide (cytoxan), Etoposide (vp16), Methotrexate, and Vincristine (vcr), along with several rescue and immune system defense agents. These rescue agents help enhance anti-cancer effects. In other words, they help prevent or lessen the side effects of chemotherapy agents.

Each chemotherapy agent may produce rare side effects and occasional side effects, but most notable are the *common* side effects, which include constipation, hair loss, mouth sores, nausea, vomiting, loss of appetite, low blood counts, loss of deep tendon reflexes, abnormal liver function tests, and hearing loss.

Chemotherapy regimens are like choreographed dance productions. As one agent flows through with one purpose, another one swoops in just at the right moment and performs its moves, in rhythm. There are villains who kill and heroes who rescue. There are key moments where each agent must appear at just the right time. If any agent fails to do their part, the entire production is shut down. It is an art created by brilliant minds seeking to solve unspeakable problems, administered by the most benevolent of hearts to the most precious of souls when there is simply no other option. Xavian's chemotherapy regimen was no different. It went something like this:

Total dose for each medication (all cycles combined):

Cisplatin 179mg/m2

Cyclophosphamide 9212mg/m2

Etoposide 576mg/m2

High dose Methotrexate 56000mg/m2

Part A

Day 1: Vincristine (VCR) 0.05mg/kg/day, IV slow push; Methotrexate (MTX) 8mg/m2/day, IV over 4 hours, given after VCR

24 Hours after MTX is given: Leucovorin (LCV) 10mg/m2/day, IV, as a rescue agent, starting 24 hours after the initiation of Methotrexate and every 6 hours until the MTX level is below 0.1 micromolar.

Day 8: VCR 0.05mg/kg, IV slow push

Day 15: VCR 0.05mg/kg, IV slow push

Part B

Day 1: Etoposide (VP16) 2.5mg/kg/day, IV over 2 hours; Cyclophosphamide (Cytoxan) 60mg/kg/day, IV over 1 hour, given after VP16

Day 2: VP16 2.5mg/day, IV over 2 hours; Cytoxan 60mg/kg/day, IV over 1 hour, given after VP16

Mesna 60mg/kg/day IV administered 15 min prior to Cytoxan and hours 3, 6, 9, 12 post Cytoxan, as a rescue agent

Day 3: VP16 2.5mg/m2/day, IV over 2 hours; Cisplatin 3.5mg/kg/day, IV for 6 hours, given after VP16

24 hours after Cisplatin is given: Neupogen 5 micrograms/kg/day administered subcutaneously (SQ), as a white blood cell booster, once a day until absolute neutrophil count (ANC) is above 1000

As you can see, precision and timing were just as important as dosage, route, rate, and frequency. The various agents played specific roles, were expected to perform specific tasks, and were supposed to exit the system within specified ranges in relation to when they arrived—what a dance.

However, rescue agents aren't always successful for a variety of reasons. In these cases, more extreme measures must be taken in order to mitigate the damage done by the chemotherapy agents.

If you had told me before then about the time you saw charcoal being pumped through an IV line into your son's body, I wouldn't have believed you. In fact, when I saw charcoal being pumped into my own son's body during his second cycle of chemotherapy, I almost didn't believe it. Even thinking about it today feels surreal. Watching the gritty black sludge slowly fill Xavian's IV line was bewildering. Those lines were usually filled with clear or yellow translucent fluid. For me, it ranks near the top of the list with a newborn baby's tar-like meconium as far as strange biological phenomena go.

During Xavian's second cycle of chemotherapy, the Leucovorin was unsuccessful in antidoting the MTX. Our medical team was perplexed, albeit cautiously optimistic, in determining why the leucovorin botched its part of the dance. Ultimately, the consensus among members of our medical team was that Cassie's breast milk, which was Xavian's primary source of nutrition at the time, was the culprit.

Breast milk is perhaps the most amazing substance on our planet. For starters, the composition of breast milk changes throughout a day as part of an effort to program an infant's internal clock, helping the infant distinguish day from night, in what is most commonly known as circadian biology. Breast milk carries this biological intelligence, and the manner in which it is created is mind blowing.

A woman's body creates breast milk by dissolving parts of herself, starting with gluteal-femoral fat, essentially her buttocks, and turning it into liquid to feed her baby or babies. Breast milk, on the surface, is best known simply as food for an infant, but it is much more than food. It's more like potent medicine that the female body has been developing for millions of years. Breast milk contains all the vitamins and nutrients a baby needs in the first six months of life, and breast-fed babies don't require water because the mother's milk provides all the necessary hydration. Nutritionally, it's a complete and perfect food, an ideal combination of proteins, fat, carbohydrates, and nutrients. Breast milk that comes in a few days after a woman has given birth contains an impressive list of vitamins and minerals: sodium, potassium, calcium, magnesium, phosphorous, and vitamins A, C, and E. Long chain fatty acids like DHA (an omega-3) and AA (an omega-6). It's very much alive and filled with good bacteria, called microbes, that keeps a baby's digestive system functioning properly. These microbes are kept alive by oligosaccharides, which can't be digested by infants, and exist to feed these microbes. It's not surprising that such a powerful, foreign agent like MTX would have trouble meshing well with such a potent, natural substance, with one agent seeking to break down and destroy cells, while the other agent seeks to nourish and program life into the body.

Xavian's second cycle of chemotherapy was botched and deemed incomplete. His body simply couldn't clear the MTX in time, thus charcoal was sent in as an absorbing agent to bring it all out, and it was successful in that. The only option was to cancel the remaining components of the regimen, take twelve days off, then try again. The realization that Xavian would likely be receiving four rounds of chemo instead of three set in, and our morale was steadily decreasing.

The toxic agents that had entered Xavian's body with hostile intent did not disappoint. A week into his first cycle, I felt a thick layer of apprehension settle heavily atop of my inherent angst. I was used to angst, but I didn't care much for apprehension, or any type of anxiety for that matter. It felt too random and confusing, and made it difficult to pinpoint what was actually going on within my emotions. I remember thinking on several occasions, "They are killing him, and there's not a thing I can do about it." Naturally, tears followed. It felt good to cry.

Xavian was feeling all the advertised effects of chemotherapy, but he was an infant and couldn't tell us if he was hurting or if he felt nauseated, etc. Chemotherapy agents don't discriminate. They are terminators in every sense of the word. They seek and they destroy. That's it. Infants don't get a free pass just because they are small and helpless. These drugs aren't concerned with how precious and innocent a child is. Our baby's body was under siege. It was an all-out attack, an aggressive offensive to decimate an aggressive cancer, and Xavian's body received every bit of the collateral damage.

During the first cycle of chemotherapy, Xavian began developing painful rashes on his stomach and around his anus, thick congestion and excessive mucus in his throat, dehydration, fever, low white and red blood cell counts, agonizing mouth and throat sores, nausea, abnormally strong gas, vomiting, painful diarrhea, hair loss, fatigue, loss of appetite, constipation, and bruising. Most of these symptoms could be seen simultaneously. Xavian received blood transfusions to help boost red blood cells, Benadryl for rashes, Tylenol and Morphine for pain, various anti-nausea medications, Zantac for acid reflux, Mylicon for gas, Keppra as an anti-seizure medication, and various antibiotics. The painful mouth and throat sores were especially troubling, as the resulting pain was so intense that Xavian stopped swallowing and eating. We had to constantly suction mucus and drool from his mouth. After a few days of not eating, Xavian received a feeding tube so that he could continue to receive nourishment.

This list of symptoms looked vastly different on paper than it did once it became part of our daily routine. The chemotherapy agents were killing Xavian, but we would soon learn it would take much more than toxic drugs to kill our son.

BURNOUT CONUNDRUM

After the first few cycles of chemotherapy, Cassie and I quickly realized that if we both tried to stay at the hospital with Xavian every single night, especially if the other rooms were as remotely distressing as *The Dungeon*, we would burnout far too quickly. Another cycle of chemotherapy was scheduled and this configuration simply wasn't going to work. Besides, we had a one-year-old, Dante, who needed at least one of his parents there with him. The last thing we wanted to do was lose our firstborn in trying to save our second born. We didn't have many options, however. Our neighbors, The Cheesemans from Wisconsin were remarkably gracious in taking care of Dante in whatever capacity we needed. Perhaps their short stint in Alabama was predominantly purposed in helping us. If that's the case, they aced it. As wonderful as The Cheesemans were, Dante needed to be with us in the same way we needed to be with him, so we came up with a solution. Cassie and I would simply alternate nights at the hospital.

Our solution, albeit a lonely one, proved effective. Cassie would be with one of our sons while I would be with the other. Neither of our children would fall asleep at night without one of their parents present. It would also give the parent staying at home a chance to re-energize enough to keep going. At the time, it seemed trivial, but thinking back I believe it paints a beautiful picture of the sacrifice a parent will offer to their children and their family when everything is on the line. I saw that same picture painted by other families who were fighting the same battle as us, at the same time, and in the same place. There's a certain beauty in that, which I've never been able to put into words, but one which has given me a unique perspective on life and sacrifice.

As we progressed through each cycle of chemotherapy, I felt like Cassie and I had become strangers in the night, exchanging a hug and a kiss on the cheek in passing. Amid our fight to keep our son alive, our marriage felt like it had been paused, at least in the sense that we were living the same life, but separated. We took full advantage of text messaging as we tried to communicate as effectively as possible. I missed Cassie though. I can't remember ever feeling as lonely as I did then. There was just something special and comforting about both of us being together at home and falling asleep in the same bed, and both of our boys falling asleep in their beds.

At home, I would lie in bed at night watching the television series *24*. Cassie would do the same when she was home. This was back during the days when Netflix actually mailed you a physical DVD or Blu-Ray disc, then you waited a day or two for the disc to arrive at your home, then you actually placed that disc in a device known as a Blu-Ray player, where the disc was read and sent to your television. Barbaric, I know. There was no streaming. It helped to pass the time, and the series was full of suspense. Not that we needed more suspense in our lives at the time, but it certainly helped relieve stress and gave us something to look forward to at each day's end.

A cycle of chemo consisted of the initial hospital stay where Xavian received his chemotherapy agents, those agents tore down his white blood cells, and once his absolute neutrophil count (ANC) rose above 1000, we would go home. That initial stay usually lasted about two weeks, but felt like two months. We would stay home until the next cycle of therapy or until Xavian developed a low-grade fever. We never stayed home until the start of the next cycle though, as Xavian spiked a fever each time. It was expected, but still aggravating as we silently hoped to stay home together for a while.

On average, we probably stayed home for two days after the initial discharge. Once Xavian spiked a fever, we would return to the hospital to have him examined. The emergency room had protocols in place for children who were on chemotherapy and spiked fevers while at home, so the process was always fairly smooth in that regard. Each return visit to the emergency room would result in Xavian being readmitted to Four Tower. This second phase, for lack of a more technical word, usually lasted at least a week and a half, but occasionally lasted over two weeks and basically consisted of a long, slow waiting game for Xavian's ANC to rise above 1000 while he was closely monitored.

Once we were discharged, we would go home and rest for a week until the start of the next cycle. Generally, we were in the hospital for three weeks each month. It was exhausting, frustrating, and left me with an overwhelming feeling of confinement, which I grew to resent. Even worse for me was not knowing how many cycles we would have to endure. Initially, only a few rounds of chemotherapy were scheduled, but our medical team made us very aware there could be more. Little did they know how much they were feeding my anxiety with that bit of information.

My time spent in the hospital one-on-one with Xavian was draining. He was a demanding infant who couldn't do the things he wanted. He was constantly attached to intravenous (IV) lines, monitors, and other devices during administration of the chemotherapy agents. Add the fact that he was often nauseated and constantly urinating from being fed so many liquids, and you're left with a child who was not very mobile. Simply taking him for a walk down the hall was no small task. At times, it was simply impossible. This left me with a feeling of entrapment in a one hundred square foot room.

Some days I never left the room. Food wasn't always available and, if I hadn't brought something to eat or eaten the small plate of food allotted to Xavian as part of his hospital stay, I didn't have many options for food. There was a small store downstairs named the GO Store, which sold plenty of snacks and drinks, but there was supposed to be a parent or caretaker in the room with the patient the entire time, and for good reason, so dashing down to the GO Store was rarely an option. There was a cafeteria as well, but as was the case with the GO Store, it wasn't open very late and I didn't have the option to just walk down to it. I rarely asked people to bring me food because it made me feel uncomfortable, like I was an annoyance, so most days I just remained somewhat hungry and lived off the Sunkist drinks which the nurses so graciously brought me. Occasionally, a few friends from work or friends of Cassie's would bring dinner, and we are forever grateful to them.

Our nurses were wonderful, pouring their hearts and souls

into their job, but there seemed to be more turnover than one might expect. Their jobs were emotionally demanding, and sadly, not all kids on Four Tower went home. The men and women who were there to care for, comfort, and love their patients and their patients' families were dealt a spiritual and emotional blow when one of the kids didn't make it home. I know this because I witnessed it on multiple occasions, standing in the doorway of our room on Four Tower with my head drooping, overcome with emotion for the families. I saw and felt their pain empathically.

Our nurses were superstars. They were our heroes. I tried to make their jobs easier by not being a difficult, annoying parent. That was important to me. I chose to look at everyone as a teammate, because we were on a team together after all, and good teammates help one another. It served us well. If I had thought they were there to just do a job, I may have approached things differently, but it was glaringly obvious early in our journey that our medical team's mandate was hope-driven, not task-driven.

I can't imagine how many Sunkist drinks the nurses brought me. It's an irrationally large number, I'm sure. The small nugget ice (aka Sonic ice or bullet ice) gave a cup of Sunkist exactly what it needed to help take the edge off a stressful day, although it wasn't so good on the teeth. If our nurse asked me if I needed anything, the answer was almost always, "A cup of Sunkist, please."

A DAY IN THE LIFE

Hospitals can be very depressing places, even if you're only visiting. Living in one for an extended period can be extremely dispiriting, especially if you can't find your groove. I never found my groove during our time in the hospital when Xavian was receiving chemotherapy and I paid a price for it. Sure, I adjusted. Cassie and I both did. We found a routine of sorts, but what I'm referring to is different. It's more about feeling confident that you have what it takes at the beginning of each day to conquer that day.

I never felt that back then. Every day felt heavy, like I was carrying five times my weight. As a result, each day was a tiring grind. It felt like I was eternally playing catch-up. A person in such a position *can* be successful, but they'll most certainly always feel a bit off. During our time spent living in the hospital, I needed alone time. I needed more alone time than I do today, yet the only alone time I was able to obtain was the few hours at home every other night after Dante went to bed, when I could barely stay awake myself. That doesn't really count as alone time. My mind needed the time, not my body. It wasn't enough, and as time went on, it affected me greatly, in a very negative way.

We were fighting battle after battle, and such is the type of sacrifice one makes when they are at war. You have to find ways to win. Just like sports teams who aren't the most talented or the best coached, but seem to somehow win championships. They manufacture wins. We manufactured wins, these sort of minor victories, on a daily basis, nursing our wounds every step of the way.

The hospital came alive during the early morning hours. Shift change for the nursing staff brought more nurses in. Those same nurses began assessing their patients, checking all the boxes, plotting their plan of attack for the shift. Doctors began making their rounds. They usually wore button up shirts with ties. Sometimes they wore lab coats. The information we received from them was compendious and I was often left thirsting for more detail.

Sometimes they would show up with an entire team of students who were aspiring to make their own rounds in the not too distant future. That was always a bit awkward for me, but I understand it's a necessary part of the process. Most mornings, those same doctors served as my alarm clock as I instantly went from sound asleep to wide awake and disoriented. For some crazy reason they expected me to be tuned into their spiel for three whole minutes as they gave me information I already had. These encounters became redundant, dull, and annoying. When the doctors departed, I was left staring at the wall with watery eyes, mad scientist hair, and bad breath, hoping I could somehow fall back asleep. I was never that lucky. There was no going back to sleep at that point because Xavian was awake for the same reason I was.

The next step was figuring out breakfast. Most days the food cart came, but some days it did not. I never did figure out the reason for that. Unfortunately, they weren't bringing breakfast for the parents. The breakfast was for the patients. But since Xavian was an infant and had a feeding tube for the majority of our hospital stays, the breakfast was mine or Cassie's. If we didn't eat it, it would just get thrown in the garbage. There was never a lot of food, but it was our only option, as leaving Xavian in the room by himself or with a nurse was against the rules.

There wasn't a system in place at that time to order breakfast, lunch, or dinner. After breakfast, things would sometimes quiet down a bit and the rest of the morning would drag on slowly. I remember being bored out of my mind and feeling caged like a wild animal. Occasionally, a nurse or clinical assistant (CA) would come into the room to check vitals, change out fluids, or administer a medication, but for the most part it was quiet inside the room. There was plenty going on outside the room though. As nurses stirred throughout the morning, they scurried to and fro while caring for patients and families. They really seemed to know what they were doing, which is a good thing because there was nobody else who could tell them what to do.

Things quieted down a bit around lunch time. Nurses would take their lunch breaks, going down to the cafeteria, often bringing their food back to the unit and eating it in their break room. As it was with breakfast, the food cart would come again around noon, ushering in whatever lunch had been picked for that particular day. The food was never great, but it was usually digestible. When you're really hungry, it always tastes a little better. By that time of day, I was in the early stages of going stir crazy and my hair and eyes supported that claim. Food didn't do much to address that issue. What I really needed was to go outside and walk around for twenty minutes. On rare occasions, the pieces would fall into place and that prayer would be answered.

As the afternoon dragged on, there was a shift change where things would get a bit hectic in the unit outside of our room. There was a sort of hum, like the humming of a crowd, that would gradually ramp up, then gradually die down thirty minutes later. After the shift change, our nurse for the new shift would come in and greet us, check vitals, and make sure we were taken care of. I always enjoyed the anticipation of who our nurse for the evening would be. Some days, we got a final visit from one of Xavian's doctors or nurse practitioners. Allison was his primary nurse practitioner at the time and I always enjoyed chatting with her.

As the majority of the daytime staff left in the afternoon and the evening fell upon us, the hospital slowly turned into a ghost town. There was less pitter-patter, softer hubbub, and fewer people. Nights felt barren and a bit eerie. They were most certainly as boring as the days. Opening the door of our room and peering out onto a seemingly empty unit left me feeling insecure. The choking grip of overwhelming claustrophobia, brought on by being trapped in our small room and feeling unnerved by the ghostly halls of a hospital after dark, left me petrified and frazzled.

A hospital is no place to live, but it can be a good place to stay alive, or help keep someone alive.

NOT A CREATURE WAS STIRRING

Xavian had fought gallantly during his first few rounds of chemotherapy, but his young body was beginning to break down from the aggressive treatments. Amid struggling through painful mouth and throat sores, which hurt him so badly he stopped eating, Xavian continued to struggle with rashes, and was quickly falling behind on basic development.

Our third cycle of chemotherapy was proving difficult, albeit uneventful, and we prayed Xavian would start eating by mouth again, for no more mouth and throat sores, and for it to be the last cycle of chemotherapy he would ever receive. Our medical team appeared to have gotten Xavian's pain under control, so we finished the third cycle of chemotherapy without incident and headed home. While we were home though, Xavian began vomiting frequently and his feeding tube looked to be pushing its way out of his throat. It was the weekend and we were overcome with concern, so after a brief discussion, I took Xavian to the emergency room so Cassie could stay home with Dante and find a moment of respite.

The eighteen-mile drive to the hospital was short. The wait in the emergency room was even shorter. When someone shows up with a child who is a hematology and oncology patient, the staff doesn't play around, especially when the patient is considered "on therapy," which is just a shorthand way of saying the patient is currently receiving or recovering from chemotherapy. Once the doctors examined Xavian, they confirmed that we had made the right decision by bringing him in, as his glucose levels were low and he would have been dehydrated soon.

I wasn't used to nights in the emergency room. In fact, this was the first night I had visited the emergency room since the evening we initially brought Xavian in, the day before they found his brain tumor. The night I brought him in alone was difficult and time seemed to move at a snail's pace. It was so quiet you could hear a pin drop. It was the middle of June in 2009, and not a creature was stirring, not even a mouse. The entire place felt deserted. The waiting room was quiet, but the hallways were *ghostly*.

The mood was eerie. A cold, institutional vibe emanated from the long hallway where our room felt tucked away from anyone or anything. My old friend, the fluorescent lighting, complimented the irritating chill of the place with an equally irksome low frequency buzzing. At some point, I heard frantic footsteps in the hallway followed by what sounded like the plummeting of a metal bed pan. The echoing sound was jarring. As I cracked the door open and bravely peered into the spooky hallway, I saw nothing—nobody, only the continued humming of those headache-inducing fluorescent lights, whose nonlinear flickering added to my already elevated tension. My mind was playing tricks on me.

By that point, not only was I frustrated, tired, and worried about my son, but I was a little afraid. It was late. I was delirious, bordering on *unhinged*. I'd seen enough horror movies to know that there was a murderer silently roaming the hallways, going from room to room, tormenting family after family. Oh dear lord what a way to go. Crashing into a medical cart or dropping his weapon, or a bedpan for that matter, meant the killer was getting nervous, and thus sloppy. We were living on borrowed time. I was certain we were next. I reached for the nearest object. I was ready for this killer.

Of course, my imagination had once again gotten the best of me. Xavian was sleeping peacefully and we were safe. As I sat in our small room staring at an IV pump, I felt defeated. I was alone, my hope was waning, and I was cold and uncomfortable. I wished Cassie were there with me. I was hungry and struggled to stay awake. Gritting my teeth in an attempt to fight back tears of exhaustion, I could only shake my head in disbelief. I didn't want to cry. I had grown tired of crying. I'd cried enough during that time. Surely there was a better way to release that negative energy. Besides, it seemed like my well of tears should have been empty by that point, but I guess our bodies have an endless supply.

As I took a selfie with my Samsung Blackjack cell phone, I looked worse than I felt, like a boxer who was being pummeled and couldn't fight back, yet the referee wasn't stopping the fight for some reason. Soon after I posted my selfie on Facebook, an old friend from high school messaged me privately, expressing his concern for me and offering encouragement. I sincerely appreciated it. In certain conditions, that type of gesture is priceless. The short encounter with my friend pulled my mind out of the present and into the past for a moment. It helped more than he'll ever know.

The room was pitch black. The blue light of the IV pump offered a faint glow while a thin horizontal line of light sneaking in underneath the door reminded me that light always overcomes darkness. When we were finally admitted to Four Tower later that night, I felt immense relief. I just wanted to lie down, but the process of getting admitted was anything but streamlined. A few hours later, after Xavian and I arrived in our room, I finally rested. It was one of the most subtly stressful nights I had ever experienced.

OBSTRUCTION

O ver the next week, Xavian continued to struggle. As we approached July in 2009, he remained extremely uncomfortable. By that point, he was receiving morphine on a regular basis. Cassie and I continued to struggle as well. Chemotherapy had become more complicated and confusing in ways we could never have expected. Our medical team ran tests and a computed tomography (CT) scan showed that Xavian's right lateral ventricle in his brain was larger than a previous scan had shown just three weeks prior. After much deliberation, our medical team came to the conclusion that his cerebrospinal fluid (CSF) was being obstructed from draining properly. They were convinced this was the source of his pain and discomfort.

Xavian needed surgery immediately. However, chemotherapy obliterates white blood cells, and his white blood count was essentially at zero, which was a long way away from the normal ANC of 4,500 or higher. On a given hospital stay, after chemotherapy had been completed, we could go home only when his ANC reached 1000, but as far as any type of surgery was concerned, like a surgery which would allow CSF to drain properly from the brain, that wasn't enough. There was simply too much risk of infection. Ultimately, we would have to wait for Xavian to be healthy enough for surgery, while he remained extremely uncomfortable in the meantime.

Time gripped like a vise as its hands slowly clutched the necks of our positive outlook.

BREAKING POINT

Xavian cried inordinately. It was actually more screaming than crying. It had been three weeks since I'd taken him to the emergency room because we thought his crying had something to do with the mouth sores. Before that, we'd tried all the common medicines, Tylenol, Benadryl, Orajel, Zofran, etc, but nothing seemed to work. After a few days in the hospital, our medical team identified an obstruction, or flow issue, causing pressure to build up in Xavian's head. They believed it was related to CSF drainage, or lack thereof, but we were left waiting for surgery until his white blood cells were high enough to have a shunt placed under his scalp. We weren't getting much sleep, and we were sure no one else on our hallway was either. I remember Cassie writing in our journal how he cried all night, so she just cried right along with him. The following night, I would experience the exact thing she wrote about, in a profound way.

Things were as difficult as they had been since the day the tumor was removed from Xavian's head in February, almost five months earlier. Since we started the journey, the pressure had been constantly increasing, both figuratively and literally, emotionally and physically. I couldn't find the solitude I so desperately needed, I only saw Cassie in passing, and I felt like an alien in a foreign land who had lost contact with the mothership.

It was a drab Friday afternoon. I left work at 5pm that day and headed straight to the hospital. Work wasn't going well. I wanted to quit so badly, but it wasn't an option. We couldn't afford to lose the health insurance. The insurance coverage was average at best, and the premiums were even less satisfactory, but it was still our best option at the time. It was immensely better than not having insurance at all, so I sucked it up and remained employed. I wanted to go home, but Cassie needed a break and it was my night to stay with Xavian.

When I arrived at the hospital, Xavian was screaming. He had been screaming all day and our medical team was scrambling to comfort him. I knew Cassie would most likely need to leave promptly upon my arrival, so I prepared myself mentally to take over immediately once I arrived.

For the next six hours, Xavian's condition worsened as he

continued screaming, unable to find comfort. My condition worsened as well. Like Cassie before me, I was unable to fight back tears, even with our nurses and medical team in the room. As I sat down on the firm fold out couch with my hands over my teary eyes, one of our nurses spoke to me, but my mind drifted far away. I could hear her speaking, but I couldn't understand what she was saying. It wasn't a conscious decision, but I had drifted off to a tranquil scene where I sat on a hillside overlooking a beautiful stream running through a peaceful prairie.

Something was wrong with me. Surely I was dying. Less dramatically, I was probably just extremely stressed, but it's what I imagine dying would feel like. I was overcome with emotion as my head throbbed. My heart raced erratically. I was nearing a breakdown. Our nurse realized how badly I was struggling, and the fact that she noticed amid such chaos speaks directly to the magnificence of our nurses.

Xavian continued screaming. I was trapped in a sphere of chaos, losing control, and drifting further from reality. I had become momentarily incapacitated and our nurse knew I was breaking. However strong I thought I was at that moment was inconsequential. I wasn't strong enough. Our nurse sympathetically advised I leave the room and the hospital, take a walk, and find a place to relax and catch my breath, so I did. Patients aren't supposed to be left unattended by a parent or guardian, but it was necessary and I'm extremely grateful for such a caring, pragmatic nurse who recognized a need and acted upon it accordingly.

As I exited the hospital, I immediately felt the first layer of stress lift. The fresh evening air aided and escorted me toward revival, acting much like a trainer helping an injured football player off the field. I found a bench a few hundred yards away from the hospital, somewhere on the UAB campus near an immaculate grassy field. The night was mild, at least in relation to a typical July night in Alabama. There was a nice breeze. The wind darted playfully.

I slouched, scared and desperately probing my mind for answers which could not be found. My teeth pressed down on my lip. I stared straight ahead into nothing. Tears poured out of my eyes until there were no more. I felt so alone and helpless. I found a few more tears, but they quickly dried up. My typically busy mind was void of thought. I just had to keep breathing as my head throbbed. That was survival. I was fighting a losing battle, but fighting nonetheless. I was beaten down and broken, fearing for my health as I desperately held on to any semblance of parenthood that remained in my essence.

Once I arrived back in my own dimension and my breathing felt a bit more normal, I slowly stood up from that downtown bench, stretched my legs for a moment, then took a long, slow walk back to the hospital. By the time I returned to our room after being gone for almost an hour, I found Xavian lying calmly in his bed with a nurse by his side—a scene which would have solicited additional tears had there been any left. With my head still pounding, and fear slowly withdrawing, I lay down on my bed, which was essentially just an uncomfortable couch, and I slept.

SHUNT

O nce Xavian's ANC came up a few days later, it was time for surgery to determine exactly what was blocking the CSF drainage. The surgery went according to plan. The diagnosis was Hydrocephalus, which is a condition where fluid accumulates in the brain, commonly in young children, enlarging the head and sometimes causing brain damage. The shunt placement brought Xavian much needed respite. It brought Cassie and I mental, emotional, physical relief, and respite of our own. We weren't sure if the shunt would be permanent, but we knew it could be.

After a few weeks of recovery from the shunt placement surgery, as well as rest from three and a half grueling cycles of chemotherapy, we visited our neuro-oncologist. She was pleased with Xavian's weight gain, but then informed us that she wanted him to receive at least three more cycles of chemotherapy. Considering we were going to that clinic visit with the hope that he might not have to receive any further chemotherapy, we were severely disappointed. But we understood the battle we were in, and by that time we were already battle tested, so we sucked it up and prepared ourselves for the next three rounds, hoping and praying it would go more smoothly than the previous three. We were most definitely ready to be finished with chemo, as well as life in a hospital, but we were fully committed to killing all the cancer in Xavian's body. So, we once again signed the dotted line of the chemo contract and geared up for battle.

NO EVIDENCE OF DISEASE

O nce Autumn of 2009 rolled around, the heavy humidity and oppressive heat of an Alabama summer headed south, making way for mild temperatures and happy hearts. The cool, refreshing air of Fall injected life into our souls. As it did every year, Autumn brought with it something inexplicable, a certain smell in the air which tickled the soul and sprayed a nice puff of hope into everyone's spirits. Just as the smoldering summer sun was sure to end us, with the snap of a finger we awoke to mysteriously fresh conditions and caught a second wind. As resilient as humans are, our moods are vulnerable.

The residual cancer in Xavian's brain was responding well to the chemotherapy treatments, according to scans taken a few weeks earlier. The remaining tumor was shrinking and the medical staff were pleased with the progress, so we forged on. We only had a couple more scheduled cycles of chemotherapy.

The final few cycles were uneventful, aside from the fact that one extra cycle was appended to make sure all the cancer was indeed annihilated. By the time Xavian's chemotherapy was nearing the end, we felt like we were part of the family on Four Tower. Our medical team knew how to best interact with us and we knew what to expect from them on a daily basis. Cassie and I continued to alternate nights at the hospital for three weeks each month, while spending much needed time with one another at home for the other week of the month.

By late November, after we had finished our last scheduled cycle of chemo, we anxiously awaited word from our medical team on whether or not the residual tumor had been completely destroyed, or in technical terms, whether or not there was no evidence of disease (NED). At that point, we had two big fears: 1) some residual tumor remained and we would be required to go through more cycles of chemotherapy or radiation; and 2) worse, the cancer had stopped responding to chemotherapy altogether and had once again begun growing.

As fate, or perhaps grace, would have it, the results from the scan came back as NED. Like prisoners at the end of their sentences, we had been released from our shackles and were free to pursue a normal, boring life, just like everyone else. Like the character Kevin Flynn said in the movie *Tron: Legacy*, "Life has a way of moving you past wants and hopes." For a moment, we had moved past the normal wants and hopes of life, and were open and excited about the concept of a boring, uneventful existence. We were going home and we had no desire to return to the prison where we had been held captive for nine months. We were over it. Done.

Nothing clouds a mind the way success does though. The fight was still in the early stages, yet our opponent had already landed several deleterious blows, leaving us stunned and a bit befuddled. What felt like the final bell of a twelve round duel was actually just the beginning of an earlier round, not even halfway through the fight. We had a long way to go. A knockout seemed inevitable.

SUFFERING AND COMFORT

I f ever there was a time in my life when I was suffering, it was during the Summer of 2009. I was broken down in a way I'd never been broken down before. There's no doubt I had faced trials in my life before that point in time, but it was different; it wasn't really about me. It felt less like a dramatic crisis and more like pure, genuine suffering with the life of another human, my son, on the line.

In the Netflix Film *Jim and Andy: The Great Beyond*, which is one of my favorite films, Jim Carrey speaks about his childhood and how his grandfather treated his father, saying, "All that pain was so valuable. Suffering is so valuable." The part about suffering being so valuable resonated with me on such a deep, personal, spiritual, yet very practical level. As someone who struggles to find comfort in comfort itself, I often find comfort in things like pain and suffering, and when I heard Jim Carrey speak those words, I was overcome with emotion. Goose bumps rose from my skin like a freshly watered plant in sunlight. Tears welled up in my eyes, and ran down my face like a slow-moving, shallow stream. Wow. I genuinely understood where he was coming from and knew exactly what he was speaking of.

I dislike the constant tugging of comfort on my soul and I often struggle to delineate between accepting comfort for what it is and avoiding discomfort. When I think of each person in the world who doesn't get to enjoy the comforts I do, I feel enormous guilt. They were created and born just like I was. They eat and drink just like I do. They fatigue just like I do. They breathe just like I do. They suffer just like I do. They are human just like I am. Someday, they will die—just like I will. What gives me the right to have more than them? What gives me the right to find warmth in the frigid cold and to feel the relief of cool air in the oppressing heat? The answer is nothing. Nothing gives me the right.

Either through some innate yearning deep within my soul or due to being heartbroken over society's epic failure as a whole, comfort is something I find myself at odds with. I constantly, freely, and knowingly allow myself to be put into positions where I am uncomfortable, and I often thrive. However, at times, I desperately indulge in comfort, feeling little control over my body, spirit, and soul. It becomes a frustrating mental tug of war.

Suffering is not a bad thing. I think about it often. In fact, I've never met a person who didn't suffer in some way, which leads me to my next thought: why do we run from it so frantically and face it so apprehensively? Suffering is part of our existence. There is something otherworldly about it and there is something in it which connects us to an afterlife. Perhaps this is where comfort plays a role. Is comfort at war with suffering? I can say for certain they are at war in my life.

Any time I'm able to put comfort on the bench, suffering becomes a tool for me, not something that hurts me. Whenever comfort insists on benching me, and I oblige it, suffering wreaks havoc throughout my very being and into the external sensory world around me. It's about becoming self-aware while you're in discomfort, feeling past the discomfort, or through it, into the purpose of it all. Profound meaning lies waiting to be plucked from the pain. Just like with any learned skill, it's something you have to practice each time discomfort finds you. You have to stand against the discomfort instead of giving in to it.

Pain is synonymous with suffering, but I see pain as a key. With this key, as with any key, you can unlock something, because that's what keys do, they unlock things. One thing, perhaps the most important thing, you can unlock with pain is courage. Courage removes barriers. It clears a path between the things we possess the ability to achieve and where we currently reside. Often in life, we must obtain multiple keys and unlock multiple locks to reach our maximum potential. We must suffer in order to obtain those keys and we must accept the pain to use the key in unlocking the courage.

Life is not designed around comfort and we are not designed to remain in comfort. In fact, discomfort is the very core of this entire concept. I believe this is exactly what Jim Carrey was alluding to in his interview in his *Great Beyond* movie. I feel like I could write an entire book about my perspective of pain and suffering, and hopefully someday I will. We don't often think of things in life as being both painful and beautiful, but I like to think that the most painful things in life are by far the most beautiful. When I think back to my journey as a father through Xavian's chemotherapy treatments—life in a hospital, separation from my soul mate, and facing the ultimate vulnerability—there lives a deep pain, but also an indescribable *magnificence*. There's something bold and beautiful about accepting the discomfort bestowed on us in such a tour of duty.

The challenge, of course, is getting into the train of thought that discomfort is good for us and can't harm us, although we feel like we're being suffocated by it. Achieving this mindset is tricky, especially during the storm. Discomfort is skilled in sneaking up on us and turning our minds in a certain direction. Before we know it, we're neck deep in quicksand. It's never as easy as we wish it was.

INCAPACITATED

When speaking of pain, the first thing that pops into my head are migraine headaches. A migraine headache, also referred to simply as a migraine, is defined as a headache of varying intensity, often accompanied by nausea and sensitivity to light and sound. If you've never experienced one or cared for someone who suffers from them, allow me to place a great deal of emphasis on two words from the aforementioned definition: 1) intensity; and 2) nausea. I can speak to migraines as if I've experienced them because Cassie suffered from what I would categorize as chronic migraines. While approximately 12% of the population experiences migraine headaches, chronic migraine occurs in only around 1% of the population. Cassie was most definitely included in this 1%.

Now, more than fifteen years into our marriage, I can wake

up in the middle of the night and sense, at a reliable rate I might add, whether or not Cassie is going to wake up the next morning incapacitated and unable to get out of bed and function. Her migraines are completely debilitating and have lasted up to 72 hours at a time. We've even taken trips to the emergency room because of them. When a contumacious migraine goes on the attack, Cassie is confined to a dark, cold room for the remainder of the day most times. Occasionally, her medicine works quickly. Sometimes, it doesn't work at all.

Whenever she gets a migraine, my blood pressure skyrockets. I typically have to go into a quiet room for a moment and psych myself up before I begin my shift as a single parent. There's a reason for this. I don't want to just parent my three kids. I want to do it well and I want my kids to feel safe and loved. When the stress of knowing Cassie is hurting and essentially helpless couples with the fact that I am thrust into a lone position of playing the equivalent of a doubles match in tennis without a partner, it can be completely overwhelming.

Migraines don't discriminate. They don't do background checks. They don't look at race or creed. They don't check to see how much stress or heartache someone has in their life. In Cassie's case, migraines didn't ask if she was enjoying her stay in the hospital as a mother of a child fighting cancer. They never asked if she had anything left in her tank after pouring out her entire being into keeping one son alive and another son cared for, all while desperately trying to remember what it was like to see her husband for longer than five minutes in a day. They didn't feel it was necessary to make sure she was prepared to receive the sudden and unwanted torment which they were ready and willing to inject.

Migraines don't show grace. They are unrelenting, and while Cassie and I were facing all the challenges that come with being loving parents of an infant going through chemotherapy, her migraines chose to stick around and harass us. Perhaps misery really does love company. A few times, I had to stay at the hospital with Xavian for two nights in a row. I know two nights in a hospital doesn't sound like much, but it was absolutely exhausting. Our method of alternating nights with Xavian proved highly effective, but it was designed for one parent to stay one night at a time. Other times, friends, family, or a member of our superstar nursing staff helped care for Cassie. She never had to prove her resilience and strength to me. I never asked her to, but she proved it anyway.

THE DESERT

*T*he torrid road offered maximum grip to melting tires as we drove through a thirsty desert bowl. The mood inside the vehicle was serene. The radio was off, windows were down, devices were tucked away, and every book was closed. As the protector, I focused on the road and kept an eye out for danger. As the nurturer, Cassie tuned in to our emotions, kept a cool head, and prepared to provide comfort in an instant. Our oldest child, our son Dante, offered up logical explanations and practical conclusions, while our free-spirited, youngest child, our daughter Larkin, exuded creativity with an ever-adapting enthusiasm. Our bold, imaginative middle child, our son Xavian, was with us, but in spirit only. His absence marked a clear deviation in energy and a subtle shift in dynamic. With each revolution, the tires shed micrograms of skin, as the hot road chafed like sandpaper. Just as our pain was slowly softening, our scars were *haplessly hardening.*

We came upon a small, quaint diner which stood isolated on a long, straight, dusty desert road. From a distance, it lay tucked away, as inconsequential and insignificant as any old creosote bush. With not a cloud in the sky, one hundred degrees felt like one-fifty. Distant, bald mountains peppered with green brush created an all-encompassing boundary around us. The sun lorded over the place like a guard in a maximum security prison watching over the yard. It gave the impression that no one could escape this place. The air was dry and thin. We exited our vehicle in synchronicity, if not slow motion. Each door shut at the exact same millisecond, harmoniously. Sand blasted our faces as we approached the diner like a band of outlaws converging on a bank.

A tall, thin, beautiful brunette waitress wearing tight jeans and martin ankle boots waited patiently to serve a family of four—us. She was kind, pleasant, and very warm. Her name tag read "Evelyn," but she said we could call her "Eve." The diner was spotlessly clean and the sweet smell of the blueberry pie cooling on the counter accented the savory scent of fried batter. The powerful voice of George Michael projected pleasantly from the old jukebox in the corner. His teacher had told him goodbye and he wanted just one more try.

We had our choice of any seat in the place. Seating four was easier than seating five. Dinner for four instead of five was a new and foreign feeling that symbolized the beginning of something different.

Xavian had been our spark, but he was gone and we had to learn how to be a family without him, so we headed west. It felt strange and empty. Xavian wasn't at home with a sitter. He was just—gone. We wouldn't be seeing him in two hours. He wouldn't be coming back to us. Dinner for four included grief and heartache with a side of loss. There were plenty of tears to drink. Who needs real food at such a time anyway? During the meal, quiet contemplation took the place of discussion. None of us knew what to say. There was nothing to discuss. There was plenty to feel though. And we did. We all did. It was written on our faces. Confusion on the faces of our children seemed to light the fire of humility.

We finished our meal and walked outside into the small, empty, dusty parking lot whose boundaries had been breached by peninsulas of sand being tossed in by angry winds. Parking spaces sandblasted by mother nature had lost their purpose. Tumbleweeds strolled by like stray cats hunting mice. As my family climbed into our vehicle, I paused. I stood still, facing that lonely road, looking up to the midday sun and closing my eyes. Despite its intensity, the heat was comforting. In fact, that sphere of plasma, parked ninety-three million miles away from us, provided the perfect warmth. It was where it needed to be, just as we were where we needed to be.

I walked out to the edge of the road and peered curiously across it toward the mountains in the distance, which seemed much closer than they had earlier. Their shadows were longer. It was eerie how quickly they had grown from when we first arrived. The angry mountains seemed to come alive with intent as the sand-laden wind blew right through my soul. Still, it was the sun's immense heat which kept my attention. Saguaro cacti filled the flat, dusty space between the mountains and the road. All of the cacti stood strong, thirty feet tall or taller, each with their left arm smaller, wilting, and pointed toward the ground while their right counterparts pointed to the sky, flexing their proverbial muscles.

As the wind grew heavier and more panic'd, I turned to the diner. It was gone, vanished, as if it never existed. The parking lot had turned to sand and I was standing in it up to my waist. I felt my family's presence, but I could no longer see them. I couldn't see much of anything. I just stood there motionless, in nothingness, contemplating the mountains, the cacti, and mostly the sun, until I was completely buried under the sand.

ASLEEP

The cool winter air felt refreshing. Sound moved much more swiftly through the thin air. All the leaves had fallen to the ground, so they could no longer deflect the sound as it blew by. The grass had all turned brown. Halloween and Thanksgiving were behind us, so there was a Christmas-like mood all around. It was December of 2009. Xavian had just spent almost the entire first year of his life in the hospital.

At this point, any questions directed my way on what it was like to have two small children could not be answered. Our situation was not typical, and almost everyone we knew could not relate to our situation, just as we could not relate to theirs. I struggled to find the words to explain things to anyone who asked. At the time, I don't think we were at a high enough altitude mentally or emotionally to truly measure the gravity of what we and Xavian had just been through. The entire experience was just too prodigious, and when it ended, I was stupefied. I was experiencing some major psychological shock.

The time between December of 2009 and February of 2011 is what I remember least in our entire journey. It was a dead time for me emotionally, a time when I couldn't cry. Metaphorically speaking, I was asleep. I struggled to focus on anything and wasn't exercising much. I was collecting a paycheck at work from a company with which I had little voice and even less energy or desire to fight the battles which needed to be fought. The company was crumbling and I was too. Not surprisingly, less than four years later I would quit my job at this company without another job to step into. That's how badly I needed to leave that place.

Most importantly though, I wasn't giving my marriage the attention it needed. Cassie and I had just navigated Hell in parallel, but apart, and without a map. We were exhausted. Making it out of there was sublime, but I believe we were each left with some degree of trauma. I know I was. How could a person who had just experienced such a thing not be traumatized?

Life was difficult and disconcerting for me following Xavian's chemotherapy. The best comparison I can give is that of a soldier who has come home from war and feels completely out of sorts. I talked about being unable to cry for years at a time. This was one of those instances. At the time, I didn't realize how deeply I had been affected and how drained I truly was. Any energy I could muster was synthetic. By that, I mean it wasn't genuine or natural. I had to produce it somehow. It's very hard to explain.

In a nutshell, I was empty inside. I was beaten down—*defeated.* It put a strain on my marriage and essentially every other relationship in my life, but it wasn't pronounced. In fact, this manifestation of trauma within me was inconspicuous. Only now, many years later, am I able to look back and see how profoundly affected I truly was. I was really messed up. I can remember moments where I would hear Xavian screaming and crying. Only, Xavian wasn't there. In fact, nobody was there. It was just me, and I was fully aware it was just me and none of it was real, but I couldn't make it stop. It was such an overwhelmingly eerie experience. But I am strong, and I fight. I always fight.

The thing is, whenever you have kids and you're truly parenting those kids, you tend to put your head down and go to work. Parent Corporation doesn't really give bereavement or paid time off. I think this played a major role in my inability to see how drained I had become and how empty I was. I needed a month alone in the wilderness, but that wasn't an option. Parenting doesn't work that way. My natural reaction was to put up walls and close myself off. This was something that happened subconsciously for me. I don't recommend it, so if you experience this type of trauma, I highly recommend getting help. If you don't, you will suffer, and everyone around you will suffer to some degree. There's also the question of honesty. Are you being honest with yourself? It's perfectly fine, in my opinion, to admit that you just went through war, you're traumatized, and you need help. Be honest with yourself. The earlier you are honest with yourself, the more expediently healing can begin.

I've always been someone who appreciated recognition. Whether I was being recognized for doing something positive or for not doing something negative, like missing school, I always took it to heart and appreciated the fact that someone else noticed. It made me feel worthy. I've always struggled with self-worth. In fact, I still struggle with that very thing today on a very deep level. The thought that I'm merely one of almost eight billion people on Earth can instantly drive me to question my very existence and my worth altogether. I long to make a profound impact in this world, but being 0.0000000125% of the population always gives me the feeling that I really can't make much of a difference. I won't even get started on the short timespan we spend on Earth. These are just a few of the things existential crises are made of.

During those nine months of chemotherapy and the years following, I struggled mightily with self-worth. Time after time, friends, family, or just anyone really, would ask Cassie how she was holding up without acknowledging me or the major role I played in the same fight Cassie fought. It dealt a crushing blow each time and made me feel even more worthless than I already did. I had suffered too and I wanted to know that someone noticed. I wasn't asking to be anointed. I was longing to be appreciated. I craved the feeling of worth, but so many times I just had to stand there and smile. I absolutely appreciated the fact that people cared enough for Cassie to check on her and support her all the same, but this was a family effort, a team effort, and I was the best relief pitcher in the league. It was a major struggle for me as a sensitive, intuitive father who was running out of fight on the inside. It made me put up more walls and move further into my cave. I knew Cassie appreciated me though, and that alone saved me from the cold, dark sadness that awaited my arrival at the innermost corner of that dreadful cave.

A NEW ENEMY

Xavian had beaten cancer. He was a survivor. We even put together a Relay for Life team in his name. I gave a tearful, emotion-filled speech to a bunch of strangers just before the event, then we walked all night. But we were now facing a new enemy which we knew little about. This enemy was called "Special Needs" and we weren't prepared for it because there was no handbook or map for such a thing. Plus, Xavian's case was so unique in and of itself. Special needs come in all shapes and sizes and place different strains on each family that faces them.

Our flavor of special needs centered around mostly mental challenges with some physical issues. These included but were not limited to hemiparesis, inattention, anxiety, impulsivity, behavioral problems, defiance, and most prominently, OCD. Xavian had fallen far behind developmentally, both mentally and physically.

While other kids were at least pulling up on and scooting along couches and chairs, some even walking at one year of age, he was still working on sitting up on his own. Early on, it was extremely difficult to identify the anxiety, and to some extent the defiance, because many kids between the ages of two and four struggle to express themselves verbally, which can make anxiety difficult to spot. Many kids in that age range also struggle with inattention, hyperactivity, impulsivity, and defiance. I'm sure you've heard of it. It's called the Terrible Twos and it can last far beyond two years of age, especially when there are underlying issues or lack of parenting. We could see Xavian's behavioral issues developing, but it was really too early to designate them as such.

After a time, it became clear that behavior was quickly becoming a major hurdle in Xavian's development. He was also left with hemiparesis on the left side of his body due to the trauma dealt to the right side of his brain by the tumor and subsequent surgeries. He would need a great deal of physical and occupational therapy.

While Cassie and I certainly shared concern about Xavian's lack of progress, our motivation for that concern wasn't derived from fear, and we didn't care what anyone thought of us or our situation. We were focused on our family.

When you don't care what anyone thinks of you, you don't

set faux expectations for yourself or for your significant other. This allows you to be genuine. When you are genuine, people notice and, more times than not, they reciprocate. They certainly appreciate it. My favorite people are genuine people. I can't tell you how many people I've met who set completely unattainable expectations for themselves by being disingenuous. They are the most miserable people I know. I don't fault them, however, as these things usually start in childhood, then lay low, disguised and ready to strike in adulthood.

Cassie was diligent in her networking on social media with other parents, usually moms, whose children had been through similar trauma as Xavian. Most of the people in those groups were great, but there was one highly...uninformed...person, who said, adamantly, that brain tumors were not as bad as other types of cancer because other cancers stay with you, but with a brain tumor, the doctors just remove it and life goes back to normal. Believing that is one thing, but stating it publicly in a group or forum to parents who have children who have survived brain tumors and are facing *major* behavioral and physical problems, not to mention possible secondary cancers caused by radiation or chemotherapy, is another.

That's the type of ignorance we often deal with in our uninformed society, unfortunately. In a breath, society tends to be impolite and uneducated, just as that person was. I've never been a fan of comparing my hardships with the hardships of others. That's a vicious cycle which can prove quite difficult to escape. I don't recommend it. I have no problem discussing the technical aspects and implications of fighting various cancers and other diseases, but the moment any single family or person's battle against a life-threatening disease becomes diminished in any way, I consider it a critical breach of a fragile boundary.

Whatever plans we had for getting back to a normal life, whatever a *normal life* was, would have to wait. Cancer may have been in our rearview mirror, but Special Needs was on the come up. If that alone wasn't exasperating enough, other major, unanticipated battles would soon emerge.

HICCUPS

In February of 2011 we celebrated the birth of our beautiful daughter, Larkin. We didn't plan to have another child, but approximately ten months earlier there had been a slight miscommunication between Cassie and myself with regard to birth control. To make a long story short, I thought Cassie was taking birth control, but she was not. When we found out Cassie was pregnant, I thought I was going to be sick. Our life had no more room for another child, especially with all the attention Xavian was demanding. Two kids were manageable, but three kids seemed impossible. I know the math in that equation doesn't really look logical, but that's how I felt nonetheless. It's amazing how illogical we can become when we're carrying enormous amounts of weight on our shoulders.

Ultimately though, once Larkin arrived we were overjoyed.

We had a beautiful daughter to go with our two wonderful boys, and from the beginning it felt so different. Girls are very distinct from boys, even when they're babies. Parenting three kids proved a lot more work than two, but by the summer of 2011, the life adjustment was going well. Even though Xavian had many more needs than a typical child, we were beginning to settle into our new family configuration of five.

Of course, what would life be like without a ridiculous, unnecessary injury—like a concussion? No, the injury wasn't Xavian's or either of our typical kids', and it wasn't Cassie's. In late June in 2011, I was the one who suffered a severe concussion, the kind where you vomit, stay in the hospital, and can't sit up on your own. It had been an extremely dry, hot summer in Alabama. My friend Tommy and I were en route to ride our motocross bikes on a nearby track that sat tucked away atop a mountain, amongst the trees, on a plot of rolling hills.

The temperature was over one hundred degrees, and the humidity was high. The sun beat down on us with reckless abandon. It felt like the ozone layer was completely gone. For some reason though, it didn't seem to bother us that much. Riding our motocross bikes had rendered us kids in a candy shop. You know, those kids who get so excited about something that they ignore the entire world around them for irrationally long periods of time?

That was us.

This particular track could not be irrigated due to its secluded location in the middle of treacherous terrain. The result was a track that consisted of dry, powdery dirt, which was as slippery as glass. Underneath the dirt sat large, unforgiving boulders. As we set out on our ride, we agreed we would take it easy that day. There was nothing to gain by pushing the envelope. For a couple of laps, we did. Then it happened. I got crazy. A few laps later I crashed going around a simple, sweeping turn. A *child* could have gone around that turn, but not me. I crashed.

Normally, I would have gotten up and kept riding after hitting the dirt, but that day there was no dirt, only rock. As the front-end of my bike washed out, I was slammed into the rock. The left parietal ridge of my head, inside a helmet of course, pounded the ground violently. Although damaged and essentially unusable from that point forward, my pro-style helmet saved my life that day. I still remember the jolt. It felt like being on the receiving end of a Mike Tyson uppercut.

There are moments over the following hours where my memories simply vanished. Tommy told me later I was talking but not making any sense. I was speaking in a normal voice but recollecting things that hadn't actually happened. I was rambling on about how I had crashed on another part of the track. It's a very scary thing to think about. Tommy and the other riders quickly realized something was terribly wrong.

I remember coming to consciousness to the smell of cigarette smoke. I *loathe* cigarette smoke. My head throbbed. The heat seemed to be clenching my throat and my mouth was as dry as a desert. I remember feeling thirst like I never had before. Not feeling confident about my situation, the guy who was running the track that day, The Smoking Man, called an ambulance. I continued slipping in and out of consciousness as we awaited the paramedics. Upon their arrival, they quickly recognized something wasn't quite right with me, so they asked me one simple question, "Would you like your friend to drive you to the hospital or would you rather go in the ambulance?" Apparently my response was, "I don't feel so good," followed by me dropping to my knees, prompting the paramedics to mandate I ride in the ambulance.

They must have been rather concerned about my condition, as they used their sirens for the entire forty-five-minute drive to the hospital. I was in and out of awareness for the entire ambulance ride. Once we arrived at the hospital, I remember being taken in on a transport bed and seeing the fluorescent ceiling lights pass by one by one. I remember feeling very nauseated. The next time I woke, the nurse was asking me to be still, as I was literally in the middle of a CT scan. Once the scan ended, I realized my pants had been cut all the way up to my underwear. Oddly, whoever cut my pants left them on me. It made no sense.

Still in a daze, I was sure I had not turned into the Incredible Hulk then back into a normal person, although it certainly looked like I had. Cassie was at her aunt's house a few towns south of UAB Hospital. Tommy had trouble getting in touch with her because she didn't recognize his phone number, so she didn't answer her phone. After a few attempts, Cassie's aunt suggested she answer the call in case something was wrong. When Cassie finally answered, the first thing she heard was, "Hey Cassie, it's Tommy. I don't want you to panic, but Matt took a little spill at the track and is heading to the hospital in an ambulance."

He might have been able to word that a bit differently, but Cassie has always been a very cool customer, so she packed up Larkin and they headed to the hospital. She knew taking Xavian to an emergency room would be a disaster, so she asked her aunt if he could stay with her and she kindly obliged. Once at the hospital, Cassie was not allowed to take Larkin to the room to see me, so she left her with Tommy. It wasn't long before the triage nurses in the emergency room intervened and took over as Larkin's temporary caretakers. As one might expect, Tommy was slightly overwhelmed by a baby who wasn't with her mother. Larkin was frightened when she woke from her nap and the first thing she saw was this large man. What ensued was a screaming baby in an emergency room waiting area. We had a nice chuckle about that later.

As soon as Cassie walked into the room, which felt more like a closet, I immediately and frantically asked her to find a bucket. I was about to hurl—and I'm not usually a hurler. She arrived just in time because the flood gates were opened.

All my scans came back negative for swelling or bleeding, but they wanted to watch me overnight, so I was admitted to the hospital for monitoring. After all we had been through with Xavian, and all the time we had spent in the hospital, here we were again, for what seemed like such a ridiculous reason. The diagnosis was a severe concussion. Cassie knew there was no way she and the kids could stay overnight with me at the hospital, and even though I was all alone and apprehensive about staying by myself, I strongly suggested she go pick up Xavian from her aunt's house and go home for the night, so she did.

I slept well that night. I was worried, alone, and scared, but I was brave. There was just no other option. After I woke the next morning, as I lay peacefully in my hospital bed, the nurse came in and said everything looked good and I could go home as soon as I could make it over to the couch on the other side of the room. She added that I would also need to keep down a juice box and a cup of grapes. This was great news—for a moment.

When I sat up, the room immediately flipped upside down and I crashed lifelessly back down to my hospital bed, bouncing a couple of times. I lay there in utter confusion for about five minutes as my heart raced violently and I began sweating. I was terribly concerned. "What is this, and how can I make it to the couch if I can't even sit up without the room flipping?" I nervously thought to myself. My confidence in making it over to the couch had been quickly squashed, and I knew I was in for a long day.

Six hours later, after a full day of repeatedly failing to make it to the couch, I finally reached my destination. I drank a small juice box and ate a cup of grapes, but I felt nauseated the entire time. It was a *horrible* experience. Nevertheless, I kept the food down, so my attending physician discharged me. Soon after that, Cassie arrived to take me home. As she wheeled me out and drove me home, I remained extremely nauseated. Is there any worse feeling than nausea? Perhaps tooth pain is worse than nausea, but I can't think of many others. When we arrived home, I tried to get out of her car, but hurled instead. Making it from Cassie's car to our bed proved nearly as difficult as making it from my hospital bed to the couch. Ultimately though, after repeated failed attempts, I made it to our bed and rested.

I slept peacefully for the remainder of that day, but the following morning was a replay of the day before in my hospital room. I tried to sit up and the room flipped upside down, forcing me back down to the bed. I grew more and more uneasy about my condition. Over the next four days, I repeatedly sat up and crashed back down to my bed. I was in deep distress over the notion of never walking again, or never sitting up again for that matter. Luckily, grace was on my side as the dizziness gradually subsided and I was able to sit up and subsequently walk again.

I'm sure my seemingly fortuitous brain injury in the midst of Xavian's unforeseen brain tumor and surgeries has some symbolic or metaphoric meaning. Perhaps God needed me to walk in a different pair of shoes for a moment. I believe these types of things potentially carry great hidden purpose and meaning. I most certainly won't dismiss such things as being part of some elaborate and incomprehensible plan. God works in mysterious ways, so we often have to filter life events through our intuition and allow them to float around in time while the eyes of our mind have ample opportunity to connect the dots.

DEALING WITH DAMAGE

One weekday in early July of 2011, as we struggled through the thick Alabama heat, our friend Amanda asked Cassie if she would accompany her to Target. She needed someone to sit with her five young kids while she grocery shopped. Cassie, always willing to help, obliged. While Amanda was in the store, Cassie stood between her vehicle and Amanda's vehicle while the kids all remained in their seats with the windows down and the cool air conditioner blowing. This obviously was not your normal child-sitting endeavor, but it was effective nonetheless.

A few moments into this adventure in babysitting, after Amanda had disappeared into the store, Cassie looked over at Xavian and noticed something strange. His head had dropped toward the ground and his left arm was stretched out in front of him as if he were pointing straight ahead. She paused for a moment and watched curiously. The episode lasted less than a minute before Xavian's arm relaxed and dropped back by his side, and everything seemed to go back to normal, except he looked slightly dazed. Cassie decided to keep a closer eye on him. A few minutes later, she noticed a second episode identical to the first one. She pondered whether they were seizures, since we were both well-educated on the causality linking brain trauma and seizures. Just like the first episode, the second one lasted less than a minute, then Xavian was back to normal.

Over the next few days, we watched Xavian closely. We wanted to get an idea of how many of those seizure-like episodes he was having. We didn't know whether he was actually having seizures at that point or if the episodes were the result of something else going on in his weakened body. We observed quite a few episodes, so we decided to call his neuro-oncologist, who was the primary point of contact on Xavian's medical team. The next day, we visited the emergency room.

Our doctor was concerned, but she didn't have all the information she would get from the head scan she had ordered, so in the interim she prescribed Keppra for Xavian as an anticonvulsant to see if his seizures could be treated medicinally. She felt like he was most likely having seizures, so that's the path we followed. She also ordered an electroencephalogram (EEG), scheduled one week later, so that she could understand what was going on inside his brain and get all the information necessary to formulate an effective plan of attack. So, there we were again, distraught, mostly because of our concern for Xavian's health, but also due to the fact that we imagined we'd be spending more time in the hospital.

Our task over the coming weeks was to observe Xavian and see if the Keppra was working. As the days passed by, we noticed his seizures increase in frequency and intensity, and he began having atonic seizures, also called drop seizures. He would be walking along then all of a sudden fall to the ground as if someone flipped a light switch and turned him off. Of course, this meant we would be going back to our neuro-oncologist with an unsatisfactory update. Xavian left that neuro-oncology clinic visit with a helmet that resembled a football helmet from the early 1900s. It was even brown in color like those old helmets. The only thing missing was a face mask. The purpose of the helmet was to protect his head if he fell to the ground during a seizure.

I recall one incident, before Xavian got his helmet, where our family was visiting friends across town. We were relaxing at their home. My friend and I were inside with Xavian while our wives were off doing something fun. We were watching Xavian closely, just in case he fell. Unfortunately, we weren't watching him closely enough. In the blink of an eye, he fell and banged his head on the hardwood floor. The next thing we knew, a golf ball sized knot had protruded from his forehead. I felt extremely guilty and frightened all at once. My friend, who was trained as a paramedic, later told me he came within an eyelash of insisting we rush Xavian to the emergency room. As soon as the cartoon sized knot on Xavian's head dissipated later that evening, we breathed a huge sigh of relief.

Another time, a few days after he received his helmet, I was in our backyard working on a project I'd been thinking about for a while, just trying to find a few moments of relaxation. We'd planted a Japanese maple tree a week earlier and it needed a bit more work to reach *Zen status*, so I brought in zoysia grass with the plan to surround the base of the tree with it and then line the outer boundary of the zoysia grass with natural stone. As I was cutting the zoysia sod with a pair of scissors, in order to make it fit perfectly between the Japanese maple tree and the natural stone which outlined its bed, I saw something I had never seen up to that point—Cassie in a *panic*. The sound of her voice was absolutely frightening as she blasted through the back door. I had never before heard fear in her voice. I was overcome with horror as I stood frozen for a moment, just staring at her in stupefaction. As I began to run inside, I tripped, as I often do, but this time my momentum allowed me to roll once, bounce back up, and continue running.

Olympic gold medalists would have been in awe.

I feared that Xavian's seizures had spiraled out of control, or worse, he was unconscious. I'd witnessed some pretty frightening seizures in my time, so I knew how bad it could get. Even before I got to the back door, I knew a trip to the emergency room was imminent. I made my way inside our home and simply followed the chaos until I got to the bedroom where I found a disconcerted Cassie, a *bloody* Xavian, and a confused Dante who didn't know what was going on. Although Xavian was wearing his helmet, which offered him protection from falls caused by his seizures, he was running through our bedroom and tripped, hitting his head on the corner of our platform bed, just above his eyebrow. His head was gashed wide open literally millimeters below the helmet line.

"This must be one of the unluckiest kids on Earth." I thought to myself in disbelief. The whole incident was on par with everything that had happened to him since he was born. I felt such empathy for him. As anticipated, we made a trip to the emergency room where, after a very short wait, the staff stitched him up and sent us on our merry way. What I remember most about that particular incident was not the blood or the gash in Xavian's forehead, but the horror of hearing the unmatched terror in Cassie's voice. After all, she's supposed to be the calm one, not me.

After another week had passed, Xavian had his first test,

which was a standard EEG. The technician who was performing it seemed frightfully surprised that it hadn't been ordered sooner. Results from the standard EEG showed that Xavian's brain activity was significantly abnormal, so a 24-hour continuous EEG was ordered and scheduled for two months later so our doctor could capture more information as we searched for answers.

Unfortunately, seizures weren't the only major issue we dealt with during that summer. There was also the matter of teeth. Chemotherapy during childhood often increases the risk for dental problems. These problems include:

- Increased risk for cavities

- Shortening or thinning of the roots of the baby teeth

- Absence of teeth or roots

- Problems with the development of tooth enamel

For Xavian, receiving chemotherapy before he even had teeth placed him at the highest possible risk of having dental issues.

On the last Sunday of July 2011, motherly intuition kicked down the door once again. Xavian would become extremely irritated anytime he tried to eat. He was able to eat a small amount of lunch, probably out of sheer hunger, but nothing else. That night, he awoke suddenly in a screaming fit. He seemed to be running a fever, but we couldn't know for sure because our thermometer was no longer functioning. Several doses of Motrin were unsuccessful in the attempt to suppress his increasing body temp. Cassie's gut led her to believe the problem had something to do with his teeth. It didn't make sense to me at the time, but I had seen the wonder of motherly intuition, which most certainly trumped logic, so I listened—and learned. She thought it was tooth pain. Of course, our fears of a cancer recurrence loomed as large as they always had. For a long time, Xavian was at high risk for recurrence (of cancer), so it was always in the back of our minds, if not at the forefront.

The next morning, we packed the kids up and took them to our dentist. He gave Xavian a thorough inspection, but couldn't determine if anything was wrong, although he did express concern about the situation and asked us to call him back if we didn't get answers elsewhere. Fearing Xavian may have an ear infection, we headed across town to see our pediatrician. After taking a complete blood count (CBC), taking Xavian's temperature, and performing a chest x-ray, our pediatrician felt like our son had a bacterial infection of some sort. His white blood cell count (WBC) was slightly elevated, which gave cause for concern as it related to possible cancer recurrence. For the remainder of that day, Xavian wouldn't eat or drink anything, and any attempt to get him to eat resulted in food flying across the room.

The following day, we returned to our pediatrician for a follow-up of the previous day's visit. Initially we were relieved to find, after another CBC, that Xavian's WBC was back in the normal range. Prior to taking him to the pediatrician visit, Cassie was brushing his teeth that morning and his gums began to bleed. We informed our pediatrician of this, so he inspected his mouth and noticed a knot on his gums. We also noticed swelling in his cheek. Xavian was prescribed an antibiotic and we were once again on our way home. After the appointment with our pediatrician, we called our dentist to update him on the situation. He asked a few questions about the knot on Xavian's gums and the swollen cheek. After a short hold, our dentist came back and told us he'd like to schedule Xavian for a full mouth rehabilitation at Children's Hospital of Alabama, where he could sedate him and fix everything at once. He wanted to perform the procedure in ten days.

"What? Just like that?" I reasoned emphatically. I suppose our dentist had concerns all along, but didn't want to frighten us. It all seemed a bit sudden, but we had no reason not to trust him.

We were headed back to Children's Hospital for yet another surgery, just five weeks before his 24-hour continuous EEG. Xavian's full mouth rehabilitation meant our dentist would pull one tooth, cap a molar, apply fillings to each of the remaining molars, fix a few decay-related issues, then clean and apply fluoride to all his teeth. As jarring and sudden as this unexpected turn was, we were very happy to get Xavian's teeth fixed, and elated that cancer had not returned. After we returned home that day, he resumed eating like nothing had ever happened. His teeth were fixed.

Five weeks later, he was scheduled for his 24-hour EEG. As expected, in spite of our ambitious desire for a smooth experience, the EEG did not go well. By then, Xavian was much more aware of the goings-on in his immediate environment, unlike when he was an immobile infant receiving chemotherapy two years prior. Despite the bumpy road, we were able to complete the 24-hour EEG, although we would have to wait a few days for the results to be processed and fully vetted.

While we waited, due to the intensity of Xavian's seizures, the doctor decided he should begin taking a drug called Banzel, with a dosage more commonly prescribed for teenagers or adults. He would have to ramp up to the full dose over a three-week period, but an electrocardiogram (EKG) was required before he could start the medication. To make matters worse, a technician who was attempting to administer the EKG was extremely rude to Cassie and essentially gave up in the middle of the procedure, saying she'd come back later. She apparently had never dealt with a child who struggled with behavioral challenges or special needs.

Seeing how upset Cassie was about the experience, I informed our nurse that the technician would not be allowed back in our room and they needed to send someone else who knew how to care for patients and families like ours. The technician's supervisor was contacted and a much nicer lady showed up the second time. Not surprisingly, she was able to conduct the test without issue. Isn't it amazing what a positive mental attitude will do for a person?

Several days after the EKG, we received the results of Xavian's EEG. It showed hot spots in the left hemisphere of his brain which were responding to bad signals being sent from the very small amount of right hemisphere brain matter still intact. Whenever a hot spot in the left hemisphere responded to a signal sent from the right hemisphere, a seizure would occur. Although learning that your child is having seizures doesn't necessarily sound like a victory, we were ecstatic to have answers we had so desired. Those small injections of hope amid raging seas of worry later proved to be the very definition of what guided us throughout our journey.

NEW KID

By late October in 2011, medicinal methods had proven unsuccessful in corralling Xavian's seizures. EEG results from a month earlier confirmed the same, so the Tumor Board at Children's Hospital of Alabama decided a major surgery would be required in order to eliminate the seizures. This news was especially frightening, but like we had so many times before during our journey, we put on our helmet, grabbed our bat, walked out of the dugout toward home plate, and stepped right into the batter's box. You have to understand, there was no other choice. We were either all in or we were all out. We wouldn't fight for ourselves against someone in the street with anything less than 100% of what we had to give, so we most certainly wouldn't fight for our son with anything less than everything we had. The war we'd involuntarily taken part in for over two years was once again intensifying.

After two years of life spent sleeping at home, things were about to change. In my mind, a major surgery meant a major recovery. Those things together meant nights spent at the hospital. Nights spent in the hospital meant alternating with Cassie, which meant one family living *two* lives. I wasn't a fan. This saddened me deeply, but it was different this time—more complicated. *This time*, we didn't have just one other child besides Xavian. We had two other children, one of whom wasn't even a year old yet. The anxiety brought on by this latest challenge didn't matter though, we were instantly transformed into battle mode.

Battle mode is very difficult to explain to anyone who hasn't endured prolonged trauma or stress, but I'll do my best. To those of you who have been through it, you'll know what I mean. It's sort of like when the various pieces of the Iron Man suit fly in from all different directions and attach to Tony Stark's body and he becomes instantly unstoppable. It's like that, except in our case you can't see the armor because it's invisible, but we feel it anyway. There's a certain mindset that comes with it—an attitude. It's like they're playing "Eye of the Tiger" as you walk out of the tunnel. It's a cold focus, a gritting of the teeth, and a wrinkling of the nose.

Perhaps people around us saw it on our faces in the form of courage through fire. That's how I like to think about it. Cassie gets a focused look in her eye and I follow suit. Our tolerance for nonsense goes out the window. Her care-free, steady personality turns corporate and serious. My quirky, contradictory personality turns steady and consistent. We may not be unstoppable at that point, and we may feel weak and broken, but we're ready to fight any enemy who dares approach.

The day our medical team told us they would be recommending a major surgery with hopes of eliminating Xavian's seizures was the first time in my life I'd ever heard the word Hemispherectomy. It sounded a little scary at first, and the more they told us about this invasive surgery, the scarier it became. My mind immediately went down the "quality of life" rabbit hole as it had the day we found out about Xavian's brain tumor almost three years earlier. I worried he would enter surgery as this fiery, wild kid and come out a zombie, and I told our neurosurgery contact exactly that. She just smiled and assured me no kid had ever come out of a Hemispherectomy surgery as a zombie and that the opposite was actually true. Kids' personalities seemed to be unlocked through the procedure.

There was, however, a significant risk of total or partial loss of vision. Total loss of vision seemed just as scary as zombification to me. Just the thought of either outcome ignited anxiety. One of the most significant risks, other than total loss of vision, was visual impairment where the majority of the visual field in the eye opposite the side of the surgery is lost. This includes half of the central field (foveal field), and the entire parafoveal and peripheral field on the opposite side. This is called complete homonymous hemianopia. It was a major concern of ours as surgery drew near.

As we reached mid-November that year, the day of surgery was upon us, and it was as nerve-racking as one would expect. Feeling nauseated with stomach cramps was one of my body's ways of responding to such stress. I couldn't sit still. My body demanded movement, even if that meant sitting in a chair shaking my legs vigorously, which is what I did—for hours. Our medical team's assurance that Xavian would be just fine may as well have been spoken in a language I didn't understand.

After five and a half hours of surgery, several blood transfusions, the removal of enough brain tissue to equal the size of a tennis ball, the removal of his shunt, and an hour in recovery, Xavian was resting in PICU. Being back in PICU again, almost three years after Xavian's first trip there, was painfully familiar. His beautiful, dark brown, curly hair was all gone, and his bald head once again rested against a pillow while a large bandage wrapped around his head. It wasn't the trip down memory lane I ever wanted to take.

As soon as Xavian was out of PICU, I noticed something different about him. He seemed more alert and in tune with the world around him. He had this look about him that was different than before. His personality was bursting at the seams. My fears of him becoming a zombie were a distant memory. His vision also remained intact, although he did suffer field vision loss in his left eye, as we expected he would. He seemed like a new kid. Not to mention we weren't seeing any signs of seizures, which was great since eliminating them was the reason for the surgery. What could best be described before the surgery as a cloud in his head looked like clear skies afterward. Seeing and experiencing that was exciting and encouraging, and we looked forward to learning what this new kid could do. Once again, a small injection of hope into a hopeless war felt larger than life.

A few days later, Dante and Larkin were able to visit Xavian in his hospital room. It was great to have my family together in one place again. I think Dante missed his brother a lot.

"Hurry home so you can chase me around the house," Dante said to Xavian with as much love as an older brother could give to a younger brother.

Cassie, Dante, and Larkin headed home for the evening while I stayed with Xavian. Later that night back at home, as Cassie was tucking Dante into bed, he said to her, "I want Xavian to still be my brother."

Dante was almost three years older than when we first took Xavian to the emergency room in 2009. The world most definitely looked different to him at four years of age than it did at one. I'm not sure if Dante was concerned that his brother would forever live in a hospital or if he just missed having him around. Perhaps he noticed the same change I did and simply reacted differently, thinking with child-like logic that this new kid wasn't his brother and might not be coming home.

ONE IN TEN MILLION

O n December 22, 2011, about six weeks after Xavian's Hemispherectomy surgery, and five weeks after
doctors replaced the shunt in his head following that
surgery, Cassie was changing his diaper on an otherwise typical
day. This seemed like any other nose-turning, off-putting, odor-
filled diaper change until Cassie noticed something strange. She
saw what could best be described as a tube coming out of Xavian's
rectum. Being fleet of foot as she was, Cassie quickly grabbed her
phone and took a picture of the mysterious tube.

She wasn't taking the picture to share with her thousands
of social media followers. That probably would have been a bit
strange, albeit sadly representative of today's social norms. She was
taking the picture so that someone would believe her. She knew
how inconceivable it was. As soon as she snapped the picture, the

tube retreated right back into the rectum. It was gone. I remember her telling me what happened. I stood in disbelief until she showed me the picture. The problem was that we didn't know what this tube was or why it was coming out of our son's rectum. What we did know was that we'd be taking *yet another* trip to the emergency room. We were really good at visiting the Children's Hospital of Alabama Emergency Room. A neighbor offered to keep Larkin and Dante while we were gone, but I was having no part of it. I was tired of our family being separated and spending so much time apart, so I respectfully declined. After that, we all headed to the hospital together.

Call it in, here come the Halls again.

With clear roads and no incidents along the way, we arrived in record time and quickly saw a physician. He asked Cassie to explain what she had seen, so she obliged him. Our physician didn't believe her, so as she had done for me previously, she showed him the picture. He, too, became an instant believer. I'll never forget the expression on his face as it changed from unequivocal dismissal to undeniable belief. By this time, we had collectively deduced that the plastic tube was the end of the shunt line that was in place for his Hydrocephalus. The shunt line, which started in his head, ran all the way down past his chest into his abdomen, more specifically, into the peritoneal cavity where the CSF could properly drain. It's standard practice to leave extra tubing in the abdomen to allow for growth. What we didn't understand was how it had gotten into his colon and out through his rectum.

During Xavian's Hemispherectomy surgery a few weeks earlier, his surgeon had removed the previous shunt which was originally put in place in 2009. A new shunt was placed a week after he had recovered from the Hemispherectomy surgery. The determination was made that the end of the shunt line had punctured the colon wall somehow, then worked its way into Xavian's colon to take a quick peek into the world by way of Xavian's rectum, in a most unlikely scenario.

A few weeks earlier, while Cassie and I had been playing with our kids on our living room floor, Xavian had suddenly doubled-over in pain, but we weren't sure why, and he was unable to explain the pain other than it was in his stomach. The incident only lasted a minute, then he seemed fine. We believe that very moment was when the shunt line punctured his colon. It would explain why he was in so much pain for a moment, but fine immediately afterward, once the shunt line broke through the colon wall.

I asked our medical team how we could prevent this from happening with the next shunt. I was persistent in getting my point across that this could not happen again. They informed me that such a thing was nearly impossible and would never happen again.

"But it did happen," I said as I stared at them in bewilderment. "It literally just happened." They offered no rebuttal, and added that there was a *one in ten million* chance of it happening in the first place, and that the chance of it happening again to the same kid was essentially impossible. I wasn't convinced, but I accepted those odds.

The day after our trip to the emergency room, Xavian had surgery to have an external drain placed near his abdomen. The portion of the tube which had punctured the colon was left in Xavian's body in hopes that he could pass it through his bowels naturally in a day or two. The top part of the shunt was left in Xavian's head so it could continue working. The reason for leaving these two portions of the shunt line in Xavian's body was that the physicians feared introducing bacteria if they attempted to pull out either part.

After the surgery, Xavian was admitted to PICU so he could be monitored closely for infection while starting three antibiotics. Yes, THREE, at one time. By Christmas Eve, Xavian was discharged from PICU and transferred to a regular room. We were blessed to all be together as a family in a single, private room. For a moment, we were able to take a short break from trying to digest the massive amounts of information being tossed at us by our medical team and enjoy the holiday. As an aside, Larkin's first Christmas would be spent in a hospital room.

Christmas in the hospital sounds horrible, like some sort of punishment, but as it is with everything in life, there's always a silver lining. That particular hospital stay was no different. First, there was the financial aspect of staying in the hospital. It's not cheap, but we were at the end of the 2011 calendar year, a year in which we'd had a lot of medical expenses. The birth of our daughter, a severe concussion with a hospital stay, seizure medications, a plethora of clinic visits, and a major brain surgery had thrust us past the family deductible on our medical insurance plan, and all the way over that imaginary wall better known as the "maximum out of pocket for the year." Because of that, the medical costs for the December 2011 hospital stay and everything that went along with it were minimal.

Holidays are no fun for me. I don't enjoy the feeling of confinement I get when I'm at a family gathering. I'd rather just be somewhere else. It's not that I don't like my relatives. They are nice people. I just prefer very short visits where I have the freedom to walk out the door and go home when I want. Christmas especially brings me a lot of anxiety. Christmas of 2011 was different, though, and this brings me to my second point. Our hospital stay spanned the entire Christmas holiday. This means we spent Christmas Eve and Christmas Day there, and it was great. Sure, we were confined to a hospital room, but the mood was jolly. The five of us just hung out, relaxed, ate good food, opened a few gifts, combined three couches together to make a very large bed, and enjoyed one another. Nurses visited us. Xavian's physicians visited us. Strangers visited us. It was simple and there were no expectations.

A few days after Christmas, after a series of enemas and a few other techniques, the lower part of the shunt line remained stuck in Xavian's colon. He wasn't able to pass it naturally. That left us with one remaining possibility. Surgery. His surgeons were worried about the hole in the colon that would be left behind with the removal of the shunt line. If the hole didn't close up on its own, another surgery would be required to remove a small part of the colon, followed by stitching the remaining hole. Luckily, once the shunt was removed, the hole closed up naturally with scar tissue from the initial puncture.

Once the remaining shunt line was removed, an external drain was placed near Xavian's abdomen. His CSF would be monitored daily for infection. We had hoped we could get by without having an infection, but it wasn't in the cards. Xavian's CSF showed growth of a bacteria known as Pseudomonas. Pseudomonas aeruginosa is an invasive, gram-negative, opportunistic pathogen that causes a wide range of severe infections that include bacteremia, pneumonia, meningitis, urinary tract and wound infections. It's a common nosocomial pathogen causing iatrogenic meningitis infection in CSF. Whether it was transferred by negligence, a mistake with a piece of equipment, or just dumb bad luck, the situation became a lot more serious.

2012 started with a bang. The next step was for Xavian to have emergency surgery to have the upper part of the shunt removed and to have an external ventricular drain (EVD) placed. After that, our medical team adjusted Xavian's antibiotics, discontinuing two of them and starting a new one, which unfortunately ran over the period of *one month*. Cassie and I were terrified we would have to spend the entire month in the hospital as we clung tightly to a glimmer of hope that we could go home when the CSF was infection-free. The plan at that point was to test Xavian's CSF three times a week, and once three tests in a row showed no bacteria, we would be allowed to go home.

The doctors felt it was time to determine whether or not Xavian still needed his internal shunt. We were cautiously optimistic, but being more of a skeptic than not, I couldn't imagine things having changed enough to where he wouldn't need it. Right after the New Year rolled around, tests were run and the results showed he *did not*. We were elated. We hadn't had too many victories since we took Xavian into the emergency room almost three years prior, but this was certainly a victory, and a major one at that. Not only did the removal of the shunt mean his body was working normally again, at least as it pertained to the draining of CSF from his brain, but it meant he didn't require another surgery and all the complexities and risks that go along. It also meant we wouldn't have to worry about the shunt malfunctioning, as they are prone to doing.

By January 10, 2012, three weeks after being admitted, Xavian's body was free from infection. He no longer required antibiotics, nor did he require any type of shunt. We were going home. What had initially felt like a large crater in an already bumpy road had turned into a marvelous holiday full of surprises and triumphs. It felt like a Christmas miracle.

THAT TRUST THING

O ver the next few years, things were quiet for us, relatively speaking of course. Xavian was anything but a typical child. Our schedule was filled with clinic visits and physical, occupational, and speech therapy. Anxiety-inducing MRIs were scheduled once every three months. As Cassie and I struggled with the fallout from two years of bloody battle, Xavian started to exhibit behaviors not common in most children.

As someone who is very forward thinking and future oriented, I naturally wanted to set expectations with regard to Xavian's future, as well as our family's future. We did plenty of research, but there simply wasn't much, if any, information available for survivors like Xavian. Cassie became well-connected with other parents of children who'd had the same Hemispherectomy surgery Xavian had, but none of them had been down the same path as us. Each case was unique.

That's both the beauty and the curse of such journeys. Many kids, like Xavian, truly do stand alone and distinct through their trials, but the price that is paid for such exclusivity is significant and unequivocally non-refundable. With little success in understanding what the future held for Xavian, I turned to our medical team, namely, one of the senior-most physicians. He was the type of guy who knew everything about everything and he was easy to talk to. He was an older gentleman, most likely in his 60s, always wore a lab coat, and didn't seem overly concerned with what anyone thought of him. He was more focused on learning everything about everything. During Xavian's chemotherapy in 2009, this physician and I had great conversations about things completely unrelated to Xavian's medical care. During that time, I always hoped he would come around, but his visits were few and far between. Surely he could humor me a bit, since the rest of our medical team were either uncommunicative or unknowing with regard to where our path was leading.

"Generally speaking," I started, "what can we expect for Xavian's short-term and long-term future? I don't feel like we have a good picture of what's coming next, and I'd like to get ahead of this as much as possible."

He let out a sigh, removed his glasses, and rubbed his eyes.

This reaction sparked a countdown of disappointment for me.

"Uh oh," I thought to myself as my Spidey-sense, i.e. my intuition, started tingling. I braced myself for the answers I knew weren't coming.

"I don't know," he said, shaking his head from side to side in frustration and sadness.

I could tell he wanted to give me a great answer and send me on my way to enjoy the day, but it was obvious he could not.

I looked at him, confused, and queried, "You don't?"

His mood shifted from sad frustration to bluntness and authority. "What I'm trying to say is I don't know what to tell you. There are no documented cases of a child as small as your son having a tumor that large that I know of. That, in addition to the other problems he's had, means there's just no way to tell what the future looks like. I'm really sorry."

That was the last thing I wanted to hear. He was perhaps the most intelligent person I'd ever met, and was playing a major role in my son's journey, yet he couldn't give me an inkling of advice on where we were headed. I knew Xavian's story was rare, and our medical team was working together to give him the best chance at life, but my trust took on a lot of damage that day. I didn't lose trust in any individual, or in our medical team necessarily, rather I lost trust in obtaining the answers and acquiring the confidence

I so desperately desired. I just wanted more. I needed more; more information, more direction, more confidence, more—something.

There was also a big, slimy, scary monster known as medical bills that we had absolutely no choice but to deal with. We live in a world, or at least a country, where lives aren't saved for free. That's where health insurance comes in. Health insurance is a complicated thing. I've become well-versed in its complexities due to all of Xavian's medical bills over a decade plus. Because of that, I've learned there are many hidden nuggets (for lack of a better word) that you only know about if you catch the right support rep on the right day or somehow figure out yourself through random fortune. The latter is highly unlikely and rarely happens.

Unfortunately for me, early on in this journey when I received a medical bill, I just paid it. I didn't like bills hanging in limbo, and I felt obligated to pay them early and often. That's a *huge* mistake. Never do that. Medical providers sometimes bill patients before insurance has a chance to process the medical claim. If you pay them money you don't owe, you have a small chance of getting that money refunded. I made this mistake with one medical provider in particular. Once I realized what had happened, my very helpful and friendly HR rep at work helped me try to get that money back. We spent countless hours on the phone trying to explain the situation and spark action, but our efforts were ill-fated because that particular provider's billing rep insisted on playing dumb. Luckily, we convinced them to use the money as a credit for future claims, but they certainly weren't going to write me a check. This type of thing damaged my already compromised trust even further. I lost count of how many times I called medical providers and spoke with reps who were either unqualified or unwilling to help me. Eventually, I lost trust in a broken healthcare system.

Trust is a very important thing for me. My trust is something which is hard to obtain and easy to lose, but it's a very grey area. There are levels of trust. I'm very selective in who or what I put my trust in, and if there is any sign of dishonesty or incompetence, I will lose confidence. If my trust is blatantly betrayed, I become extremely cautious with every action I take. There's a closely measured, deliberate, and fragile process of reparation that must take place for my damaged trust to be restored.

Clinic visits also left a lot to be desired. I can't imagine too many situations I have more disdain for than being somewhere I don't want to be when that somewhere is also a public place. Being in public, or as I think about it, being thrust into society's spotlight, is the last place I want to be. It's the place where I have no choice but to deal with people who give no consideration to the situation of everyone around them and think only of themselves. Sitting for hours past an appointment time raised my blood pressure, and begged the question, "WHY?" Many of the processes which were broken in 2009 when we started our journey are still broken today. Why? Most of the hospital staff were wonderful, but, like me, they are only human. They have bad days too, but spending thirty minutes offering up the same information you offered up at the last clinic visit was annoying and sometimes infuriating.

"No, ma'am, my son's social security number has *not* changed." Shockingly, I had to reiterate this on more than one occasion.

Every time I took Xavian to a clinic visit, I was forced to relive the dread from that prison, the hospital, which we'd been confined to for over ten months when we started our journey. The hospital became my least favorite place. If I was the prisoner, then assuredly the hospital was my warden.

My son's future was at stake and I had lost confidence and trust in the entire system, including our medical team's ability to provide us with a roadmap. Perhaps the craziest thing is I thought our medical team was really great, even when my trust was crippled. Such journeys sometimes demand a person stay in a fragile state of mind. I knew we were in the early, albeit already bloody stages of war, and I knew we were committed to fight until we could no longer stand, but my confidence was shaken.

It felt like we were alone, forced to rely fully upon ourselves to obtain information, to figure out which services were available for us, and to determine what our short-term and long-term roadmaps looked like. Without a roadmap, how could we adequately prepare for the future? This was not the sort of journey one just approaches willy-nilly. We knew milestones five or ten years down the road needed immediate attention and forethought. It was up to us to spend the energy so that we could make predictive decisions about Xavian's future.

My big picture, future-focused personality meshed well with Cassie's ability to stay in the moment and navigate with sound decisions. It was a nice balance that allowed us to cover a lot of ground in a particularly thorough way. If you are a parent in a similar battle as the one we have gone through, you will need to understand the system is not going to cater to you. You will have to spend the energy to find the answers you need if your child is to reach any place near their maximum potential. You have to think things through and get ahead of the game. The game is not going to come to you. You have to take it to the game. You're going to have to anticipate mine fields full of broken processes and navigate canyons void of information. Getting the answers you'll need will be more like mining for diamonds than it will be picking a ripe apple from a tree. You'll also need to make the decision to not let anyone stand in your way. This is your child's life. If something doesn't sit well with you, then there's probably more to it. Take a closer look and make sure your child is getting the best care possible.

INTUITION, MEET MOTHER

I've talked about intuition and I've talked about motherly instinct in this book, but I haven't talked about *motherly intuition*. I sometimes see the words intuition and instinct used interchangeably, but when I use the word instinct, I'm referring to more of a transient reaction. It's not a feeling, but something that is hard wired into someone. In mothers, especially new mothers, it's something that awakes from dormancy and comes alive firing on all cylinders. It's glorious.

When I use the word intuition, I'm referring to an accumulation of experiences up to a certain point. It's more like subliminal processing of information or patterns that are too complex for rational thought, so it's vetted subconsciously. It's things that are constantly learned, not something innate. I stood in awe as I watched Cassie's motherly instinct awaken, like a bear out of hibernation, when our first child, Dante, was born in 2007. In 2014, similarly, I stood in awe as I watched her motherly intuition, like exploding magic, form amazing conclusions with undeniable confidence from accumulated and combined critical information to help guide us on our journey. Pay attention, fathers. You won't want to miss this fascinating phenomenon.

In the Spring of 2014, Xavian was finishing up his second full year of preschool at the public school in our town. I thought things were going well, but Cassie had been developing growing concerns about the level of education he was receiving. She had already voiced those concerns to me only to have them fall on deaf ears. After networking effectively with other parents who had children with special needs, she had formed a clear picture in her mind of how Xavian's education needed to look. She had a good feel for what he needed and knew that he wouldn't get it where we were.

In my struggles, with what was most likely some form of PTSD, I'd become blind to the reality she was fully aware of regarding Xavian's education. It would take quite some time for me to see the bleak picture painted by Cassie's intuition. As her concerns grew, she started asking other parents in her network about special education programs at other schools in Alabama and in other states like Washington DC, Indiana, Kentucky, Arizona, New Mexico, and Colorado, just to name a few. I was not fully aware of the extent of her research into this matter, but when I learned more about it, I was just as impressed as I was ignorant. As Cassie continued to look for answers, she met with her highly-intelligent local friend, Susan, who also had strong networking skills and a great deal of resourcefulness. She was detail-oriented and knew how to dig. Cassie was looking for direction from Susan, and after a lot of discussion and a few in-person meetings, she knew exactly what we needed to do.

I'll never forget the day Cassie came home after she used her motherly intuition to populate all the variables, fill in the blanks, construct each logical block, and mysteriously work that magic.

"We need to move to Homewood," Cassie said with utmost confidence.

"Homewood? That's too expensive." I chuckled. "That's where all the doctors and lawyers live, isn't it?"

"We need to move to West Homewood and get Xavian into Hall-Kent Elementary. We can afford a home in West Homewood. I've already looked into it."

I paused. "Why West Homewood?"

"Hall-Kent is the top school for kids who have special needs. In all the accumulated rankings, they are at the top of the list."

"Is our current school not working out?"

That's when I felt Supergirl's Kryptonian heat vision burn two holes right through my chest. She looked at me in disbelief and rage. "Are you joking? No, it's not working out. Our best option right now is to move to Homewood. This just isn't going to work," she said adamantly.

Thinking back, the horrified look in her eyes is seared into my memory. It was one of those times where I realize I've completely missed that thing which was right in front of me the whole time, growing out of control like a fungus, and it was jarring. It was a fist-meets-jaw moment in slow motion, where I was violently awakened to reality and everything around me grew as I shrunk.

As is always the case with anything of importance, it took me a few days to fully vet this information and deeply grasp what she was telling me, but I came around. I wanted what was best for Xavian and our family, and I trusted Cassie. It was the most logical decision, so as soon we had a contract on our already-for-sale-home, we found a home in West Homewood, Alabama, and put a contract on it. The home we placed a contract on was similar in size to our current home. Our contract, however, was denied. Two families had placed bids on the home. Instead of taking the first and higher offer, our offer, the seller went with the family who didn't have a contingency to sell their home.

We had to keep searching. We were slightly annoyed and

increasingly scared we wouldn't be able to find a new home. Unfortunately, we were up against the clock as it was already late in June in 2014 and school would start in a little over a month. There weren't many homes for sale in West Homewood at that time as the real-estate market there was about to heat up—*quickly*. The next day, we found a place right around the corner from the first one we had placed a contract on. It was much smaller, but we had no choice but to make it work. We placed a contract and it was quickly accepted.

Ironically, the owners of the other home we had placed a contract on came back to us a few days later saying their other offer fell through. I don't like to delight in the misfortune of others, but I have to admit that it felt good to let our real-estate agent tell them we would not be buying their home. Besides, they weren't going to have any problem selling it, so it didn't matter. We had found a smaller home, but in a better, prime location halfway between the community park and the school, and later, walking distance to the neighborhood pool. We were ecstatic about our new fixer-upper. A month later we moved in.

In July of 2014, we spent our first night in our new home. We were so excited and happy to free ourselves from the shackles that seemed to bind us at our last dwelling. Our new place was literally half the size of our previous one, and our three kids would have to share one bedroom, but it didn't matter to us. Our family is not driven by what we have, rather we are thankful for who we have. Not only was our new living arrangement more than adequate, but there were important life lessons to teach through it, like being thankful and doing the most you can with what you have, even though you may have less than someone else.

I revel in the opportunity to teach my kids life lessons. I may not ever teach my kids how to hammer a nail into a board or turn a screw with a screwdriver, but it's not because I can't do those things. It's because there are more important things in life such as compassion, empathy, contentment, acceptance, and gratitude. For me, that was the biggest blessing of our move to Homewood. On top of all the other reasons, we were grateful our new home was merely ten minutes away from Children's Hospital of Alabama instead of twenty-five minutes away as we were previously. At that point in time, we still made frequent visits to Children's Hospital for a plethora of reasons, so shaving fifteen minutes off the commute was a subtle blessing.

THE AFTERLIFE

By late 2014, we had settled in nicely to our new home in our new city, a feeling of optimism within each of us. The cool winter air felt inviting and freeing. We had embarked on yet another new adventure and were so thankful for the opportunity. Xavian had just turned six and had already gone through more than most of us will go through in our entire lifetime. But what was he like? How was he doing? What did life look like for a young child five years removed from a tumor resection during infancy, nine months of chemotherapy, a battle with Hydrocephalus, numerous shunt surgeries, a Hemispherectomy, a punctured colon, a CNS infection, major dental rehabilitation, and developmental and behavioral challenges?

Xavian was a colorful child. He was fiery, impulsive, funny, spontaneous, and very unique. Being quite the jokester, Xavian loved to make up words, then have someone repeat them back to him. It was something that made him laugh, so I was always obliged to join in, as were others like his speech therapist Mrs. Hopper, who took great delight in dissecting Xavian's made-up words. I would sometimes intentionally repeat a funny, off-kilter variation of whichever made-up word he wanted me to say at the time. That got the best laughs. He also loved to repeat the words to a pre-determined person, usually Cassie, myself, or one of his siblings in hopes that the person would succumb to uncontrollable laughter. This behavior started at an early age and continued into adolescence. His list of words, or at least the pronunciations there-in, as part of a self-proclaimed made-up-language, included, but were not limited to "Inkane-thon-bon," "A-capical-peeka-tay," and "Scrick-a-pooachy."

Sometimes his made-up words made me feel like if I repeated them I was going to open an interdimensional portal to hell or something crazy like that. Sounds ridiculous, I know, but that's just one example of my colorful imagination running amuck.

As a result of effective speech therapy, provided by two of the most amazing speech therapists I can possibly imagine, Xavian was speaking well by the time he was six years old. Words were discernible, especially to those of us who were with him regularly. He preferred to be outdoors rather than inside and he loved playing in sand and dirt. I believe the dirt and sand carried some sensory value or feel that wasn't attainable anywhere else.

Xavian was hyper aware of everything going on around him. He could be focusing on one thing, appearing completely absorbed, and yet notice my facial expression and ask me why I was making that face. I've always felt like that skill was amazing.

Goofball that he is, he thought going potty on our wooden fence was the best thing since sliced bread. He would pick out one vertical section of the fence, and his goal was to make a "ghost." What this equated to was a wet area on the fence in some abstract form that he believed resembled a ghost. He would expect me to join in on this ceremonious relieving of one's self, and of course I did. I even encouraged it. This is the type of thing that father-son bonds are made of. Not only did I see it as zany, but I saw it as necessary. If you wanted to be part of our club, you had to urinate on our fence, no questions asked.

Xavian wore an Ankle-Foot Orthosis (AFO) on his left leg because his entire left side was weakened from Hemiparesis, which mostly affected his hand and foot. He walked with a slight limp and ran with a negotiated stride, but quite swiftly I might add. He was unable to open his left hand, or "lefty" as we called it, in the same manner most people could. Lefty could hold and grip objects, but only with the assistance of "righty" pushing lefty down toward the wrist, then placing the object in lefty and pushing the wrist back up to a normal, extended position. Ironically, his medical team refers to his left hand, not his right hand, as "the helping hand."

Xavian suffered high frequency hearing loss from damage to the inner ear or auditory nerve, most likely caused by the Cisplatin he'd received as part of his chemotherapy protocol. Test results have also shown peripheral vision loss on his left side, a bi-product of his hemispherectomy surgery, which is why he prefers for people who walk with him to be on his right side. The most miraculous thing I like to share with people is that he essentially only has the left hemisphere of his brain. I say "essentially" because there is a very small amount of tissue in his right hemisphere, but it's inconsequential and serves no purpose because the amount of tissue is negligible. Over the years, I've gotten the strangest looks when I've told people my son has half a brain.

When people first met Xavian, they usually assumed he was a typical kid. He was a bit smaller than other kids his age, but took growth hormone to help him stay in a normal range. He looked like a typical kid, especially from a distance, but upon further review, people quickly realized he was anything but typical. Xavian was classified as having "special needs," a mysterious, powerful word, but an uncommon one in today's society.

Xavian's biggest special need was one of a behavioral nature, although his struggle with obsessive-compulsive disorder (OCD) increased in intensity as he aged. He was extremely impulsive, especially with regard to things like people or things in his immediate sensory environment. If another person bumped into him or was too loud in some way, Xavian would react, and not in a positive way. Back then, the person in question would usually be struck or spit on. If there was something that surprised or jarred Xavian, he would collapse to the ground, completely overwhelmed by the shock.

Xavian's hemiparesis made things like brushing his teeth or wiping his bottom very difficult. Occupational therapy was ineffective due to the fact that his impulsivity and lack of self-control simply derailed the process. He desperately needed to learn an assortment of life skills, but was unable to at the time.

Through the years, Xavian's impulsivity and inability to control himself in disadvantageous situations increased, leading to moderate behavioral issues. Small tasks were difficult. They were amplified and distorted out of proportion to the importance of the task. Simple requests like, "Please put up your toys," resulted in verbal abuse, defiance, and destruction of property. Toys, clothing, furniture, walls, dinnerware, and people were all possible targets of his aggression. He also became more verbal, regularly offering up serrated phrases like, "I will kill you," "Go to Hell," or "I wish you were dead." Growing increasingly physical, Xavian began punching and kicking holes in walls and throwing hard objects.

We were instructed to ignore these behaviors as they were deemed "negative attention seekers," but that proved quite difficult and became an ongoing challenge for us. During a meltdown, Xavian would occasionally try to harm himself by banging his head on the ground. When we intervened, he would focus his aggression on us through grabbing, clawing, hitting, kicking, spitting, or biting. Our hearts grew heavy and weary as we constantly fought off resentment. After a meltdown, a new hole in the wall, or a verbal or physical attack, Xavian always displayed remorse. It was as if he did these things unknowingly, unwillingly, and uncontrollably. We expressed forgiveness and empathy toward him early and often, but it wasn't easy. Our hearts were broken repeatedly.

Socially, Xavian didn't engage with other kids as much or in the same manner as a typical kid would. Honoring personal space and properly engaging someone was something which would need to be taught. A few kids were overwhelmed by Xavian's energy while others were left bewildered. I'm sure they were taken aback by this normal-looking kid who turned out to be not so normal. It's understandable. Other kids loved Xavian and showed a great deal of empathy, taking on sort of a nurturing role. Then there were the kids who were very patient and calm and treated him like a regular friend. Always bringing tears to my eyes, those were my favorite kids.

Xavian would tend to fixate on one kid. It wasn't always the same kid, but once he picked someone on which to target his energy, that's the kid who received ninety percent of his focus for the foreseeable future. This chosen one was deemed his best friend for the duration of his spotlight upon them. Some kids would be visibly uncomfortable, while other kids embraced and accepted it. He would always keep a few other kids, who he also found fascinating, in his back pocket for when he grew bored.

Because Xavian had a big personality, he and I clashed on occasion. That's normal for a parent and their child, but the difference is he couldn't easily adapt or be reasoned with like other kids. Knowing that helped me become a better parent because I had to learn how to make it work. At times, I had to set hard boundaries and offer a bit of tough love, neither of which I'm good at.

Xavian loved to laugh and be in the spotlight. If not for the paraprofessional who was with him all day at school, he surely would have owned the title of "Class Clown." It takes a big personality to be the class clown. When people hear about holes being punched in walls, people being spit on, and verbal abuse being handed out, they think of a mean kid, but Xavian was most definitely not a mean kid. He was kind with a big heart. He was very sensitive. Whenever he hurt someone, he would always display great remorse and guilt. That's why we don't judge books by their covers. You never know what someone has been through, what challenges they are dealing with, or what emotional state they may be in. Bad people aren't the only ones capable of hurting others.

Emotionally, Xavian dealt with a great deal of anxiety. Sundays were the hardest. Aside from being a highly unstructured day, Sundays were terribly difficult because Xavian was so worried about going to school the next day. What **should have been** a beautiful, sunny Sunday afternoon full of relaxing time with family and friends was instead spent being spit on and screamed at. Sometimes we would have to restrain Xavian so that he didn't hurt himself or someone else. There was no other off-day, there were no do-overs, and Monday proved that much more difficult when Sunday was especially hard.

If you've never had to restrain your child the way we have, or been on the receiving end of their verbal and physical (though unintentional) attacks, I am here to tell you how unique and terrible of an experience it is. Our hearts have broken in so many ways I could never have imagined before our journey with Xavian.

Life after a brain tumor, plus a lot of other stuff, left us with a loving kid who was a walking miracle. He had special needs and struggles that most people can't even comprehend. He looked like a normal kid, but wasn't, and sometimes that made the daily battle so much more difficult because our expectations would frequently betray us. Xavian struggled to convey how he felt emotionally and physically. As with any child, the better we learned "his language," the better care we were able to provide to him. For us, life didn't go back to normal after surgery in 2011. In fact, just the opposite was true. Our life increased in chaos. Xavian was forever changed—and so were we.

GASPING FOR AIR

In the summer of 2019, I sat at our dining room table one evening with my chin down and my hands wrapped around to the back of my head. Xavian's behavior had been spiraling out of control for months. My mind hurt and my heart followed suit. My head throbbed. I was crawling slowly and desperately across the battlefield, wounded, but the medic wasn't coming to save me. I was alone and on my own, a soldier against time, and it was up to me to save myself. The answers hadn't presented themselves and I couldn't find their hiding place.

Only questions remained. Questions of "why" and "how long" and "for what purpose" ruled my mind. I wanted to scream, but I couldn't. There just wasn't enough energy available to me. I wanted to cry, but I couldn't do that either. I was most certainly weeping on the inside, but the floodgates were closed tightly and not even a trickle of tears could pass through. I needed tears. I wanted them more than alcohol, drugs, or any mood-altering substance. I felt like an utter failure as a parent and my stock market of worth was crashing around me.

Perception and reality were at war in what felt like the fight of the century. The scuffle was viciously unbridled. In the blue corner, standing twenty feet tall was *Perception*, which informed me I was not equipped to parent my own child—a haughty foe indeed. In the red corner, weighing in at over three hundred pounds stood the defending champion, representing the fact that it didn't matter whether or not I was fit to be his parent, I was his dad and had to do the best I could with everything available at my disposal—it's *Reality*. A bloody battle within the bloody war topped the headlines.

Nevertheless, I was overcome with sadness and, even more so, helplessness. I couldn't imagine a parent having a more profound feeling of inadequacy, but as the old adage would suggest, "There's always someone who has it worse than you." I asked God why he tasked such a weak person with such an impossible duty. God scoffed. At that moment, I felt as if I were being sucked into a black hole, stretched like spaghetti, and ripped apart—spaghettification.

Earlier that day, Xavian had had a major meltdown. Cassie and I had been spat on. Holes were kicked in the walls of our home. Hard objects were thrown in every direction. Luckily no one was hit, but the day could have turned out quite differently if someone had been. There was screaming and rage, and Xavian's self-control had morphed into violent bursts of utter chaos. He'd attempted to harm himself. Preventing him from doing so resulted in attacks directed toward the rest of us.

Our other children had been on high alert, prepared to dart out of the way at a moment's notice, and they did. They were conditioned by that point to be agile and alert during meltdowns. A quick scamper and they were in a safe place. They were well-adjusted kids. They had their moments of selfishness and irrational behavior amid their flexibility, of course. After all, they were kids and there were always lessons to be learned. I always paid close attention to their energy. It came natural to me. Sure, there were plenty of times when I missed the oh-so-obvious siren that was going off, usually because there was just so much information to sift through and perhaps no pattern to latch on to, but as a team Cassie and I covered it well. I believe, as parents, we need to pay attention to our children to such a degree that if an adjustment, major or minor, is necessary, we can make that adjustment in a timely manner before it's too late.

Xavian's defiance and behavior had reached critical mass

and everyone in our household was being affected by it. We were losing faith in our psychiatrist. We needed a psychologist, but hadn't realized it yet. Better yet, we needed a diagnosis. We knew it would help to have more intense therapy, like Applied Behavioral Analysis (ABA), but our health insurance would only cover it for Autism diagnoses, a diagnosis we did not have. Welcome to health-care in America, where things rarely make sense. We started the long, slow process of getting an Autism diagnosis, but I just kept asking myself why we hadn't done it sooner. More occupational therapy (OT) would certainly have helped Xavian learn how to function with the use of only one fully capable hand, eliminating a great deal of frustration, but again, our options were limited in that regard and his behavior was still so intense that OT wasn't really practical.

We usually couldn't go out to eat as a family, fearing we'd have to deal with a meltdown in the middle of a restaurant. I wasn't embarrassed as some might be, rather I was more concerned about ruining everyone else's meal or having someone lash out at us. That most likely would not have ended well for them; I don't take kind-ly being lashed out at, especially when it concerns my family. At times, we wouldn't even walk to the park because it seemed point-less to deal with a meltdown there when we could just deal with it in our own backyard in privacy, without disrupting everyone else's day or having to hover over our child until he snapped out of it.

On a few occasions, after we left our home for an event or for something like church, if we sensed Xavian was highly anxious or exhibiting signs of a major meltdown, we would literally turn the vehicle around and drive home. This almost always resulted in a meltdown, as we expected it to, since Xavian didn't like immediate changes in plans. But we had to learn how to assess situations and make difficult decisions, quickly. A meltdown at home was favored over a meltdown at an event, church, or a restaurant.

Sometimes Cassie and I would each take in a deep breath, put on a brave face, and go anywhere and everywhere. More often than not, this involved Cassie encouraging me or vice versa. Either way, our support for one another strengthened our entire family structure. We were at our weakest when mutual support was absent.

Our struggles with Xavian often felt like running on a treadmill, exuding tons of energy, but feeling like we weren't making any progress. Xavian was often on a mission, and anything that threw him off that mission would lead to a meltdown. He almost always displayed remorse after a meltdown.

Spending time with Xavian was, at times, quite unpleasant. We felt constrained to a certain set of rules or boundaries, which if we stayed within, things would go smoothly. If we ventured out-

side those unmarked boundaries, even for a moment, then his behavior would quickly escalate. One example of this escalation is
when Cassie or I would go hang out at our swing set with Xavian.
He wanted us to sit in a very specific place, the swing to his right,
since he had peripheral vision loss in his left eye and didn't like the
fact that he couldn't see us. We knew this, but if one of our other
kids came out and tried to sit to his right, instead of Cassie or myself, then a meltdown would erupt and verbal abuse would ensue.
Being told by your child that they're ready for you to die on a regular basis for reasons not worthy of such an attack, or for no reason
at all, weighed heavily on the soul, even though we understood the
idiosyncrasy of cognitive processes which were completely atypical.
He didn't mean it.

There came a time when I realized there were just certain
things I couldn't do with Xavian. When he was on edge, I couldn't
sit close to him on the couch or speak to him. He needed space and
I learned to grant his unspoken request. It was often a matter of
reading his emotions. There were painful times when I wanted to
be affectionate with him (e.g. give him a hug), but I knew in that
particular moment, a hug is not what he needed. In some regards
it's basic parenting and has nothing to do with special needs, but
the special needs aspect is something we could never ignore. Sometimes simple things like sitting down together at the dinner table

weren't the best for our family on a particular night, so we shifted and ate our dinner in a plethora of different formats. I also had to accept my limitations in being able to handle meltdowns, so I began spending time with him in ways which meltdowns were less likely.

The force from Xavian's nuclear explosions could disintegrate feelings at the subatomic level. I've seen the most seasoned, thick-skinned people cry because of his verbal attacks. If they weren't crying on the outside, they most certainly were on the inside. I knew this because I could feel their soul jumping out at me in discomfort.

When a child experiences such explosive episodes as Xavian has, they need space, unless they are attempting self-harm, in which case you have to intervene immediately, in an up close and personal manner, and in harm's way. Once the episode has passed, that child needs one or both parents to draw near to them, just as the sun provides warmth upon us once the storm has passed. That's the moment when a child needs their parent(s) to show them outwardly that they still love them unconditionally. That type of interaction isn't limited to children who have special needs. The concept applies in any situation where discipline has been applied. It's all about a parent building up their child after that child has been broken down, and it's essential in parenting, but basic all the same.

Xavian attended a social group for many semesters at a nearby behavioral services provider. One of the first things he learned there was the "Stop and Think" technique, which is aimed at teaching children with impulsive tendencies to pause, then stop and think about the consequences of the action they are about to take. It's a great concept, one which can apply to adults as well as children. With this concept in mind, I learned that how I responded, as well as the control with which I reacted, were as important as anything else when it came to avoiding Xavian's meltdowns. Once I began to fix this part of myself, this realization embedded itself into my subconscious. As a side effect, I started noticing parents everywhere who needed to learn the concept of "Stop and Think."

I realized how important both my and Cassie's interactions with Xavian were. Creating a positive, encouraging setting was vastly important in helping him control his behavior. The intention behind spending time with Xavian turned into putting him in a position of success with regard to his self-control, and to not push him to some irrational limit where he couldn't possibly succeed. Again, it's really just basic parenting, but for us with Xavian, the consequences of not being intentional in putting him in positions of success were grave.

I recall the summer our neighborhood pool opened. This pool came fully equipped with a splash pad and spray features, zero-depth entrance ramp (i.e. a "no entry pool") with a mushroom fountain, giant curvy water slide, lap lanes, locker rooms, and full concession and grill. This pool was no joke. It's the place you wanted to be during a hot, humid Alabama summer. Unfortunately, during that particular summer, most days it wasn't an option for us as Xavian melted down each time we went. It was anything but relaxing.

It was a constant balancing act of all the various things that could go wrong. Things like small kids wandering around haplessly, and attempting to play in the vicinity of Xavian, put the kids in immediate danger of an impulsive, nuclear reaction. It was clear Xavian wanted an ideal pool experience, but was unable to adequately communicate his needs to us. We struggled to maintain peace, walking on eggshells at the pool just as we did at home, at a store, in church, or at a restaurant.

When it was time to leave, his anxiety would rise to disproportionate levels, and ours would follow suit. There was always a meltdown, and not even his deepest desire could be used as a bargaining chip during those moments. Finding his motivation was like solving a complex riddle. Occasionally, one of Xavian's friends from school would notice him and come over and offer to play with him. He would oblige them for a moment, but he just didn't possess the social skills for anything longer than a brief interaction.

Understandably, the other kid usually got bored and left after a short period. Still, we were very thankful for those kids who wanted to naturally include and nurture other kids regardless of their abilities. Sometimes when Cassie and I were low on energy, not feeling confident, or we knew Xavian was struggling that day, we opted out of making the hundred-yard walk to the pool. The risk was simply not worth the reward. One of the most disheartening feelings arises out of the fact that something is right in front of you and you can't even touch it.

Although Xavian could produce chaos and stress, there was also a calming, curious peace about him which was unmistakable. I lived for those happy moments—still do. I often think about how difficult it is when I'm struggling mentally with a particular thing, and I can't imagine what it's like for him. The relentless tugging on his soul is undoubtedly taxing. Xavian can be incomprehensibly difficult, but never have I thought he was a lost cause. He's a masterpiece and learning his intricacies is an artform, and that is one of the things I find most beautiful about him.

DIFFERENT

For us, family life was very different from other people's. Not worse or better, just different. What is a typical family's life like anyway? Does typical mean normal? If so, what is normal? Most parents would say their families aren't normal at all, and I'm not so sure normal even exists. I think normal is just something created by society to throw a veil over our eyes. I prefer to *not* compare my family's life with the lives of others, but I admit it's hard not to.

I'd much rather look at my family's life through a microscope and find ways to optimize every aspect of it, including how well-organized we are, how much we serve and love others, and how well we manage finances. I've never been a fan of "keeping up with the Joneses," and I've often soured on families who think doing so is acceptable. Somehow, greed always moves to the forefront of such a thing.

At some point, I realized that our family was only going to work in a modified capacity, so we began making adjustments. Missing out on a particular thing, or Cassie and I going our separate ways for the evening so our typical kids could attend an event became our reality.

As perfectionistic as I tend to be, I learned early in this journey that agility and flexibility, not perfection and idealism, would serve me much better as a father. With all of Xavian's obstacles, I didn't have the option of holding tight to rigid principles, and my family's survival depended on rolling with the punches. I believe idealism has its place, but I believe even more strongly that people who aren't bound by rigidity or pithiness can overcome much more in life than those who allow those fetters to limit their potential for greatness. Those who insist on clinging to unrealistic ideals find themselves desolate and resentful.

It was important for me to learn that plans weren't really plans at all, they were desires, and that ideals could be malleable as circumstances changed. In getting myself to that point, I had to become a bit bullish in how I dealt with the pressures from anyone who sought to pull me in a particular direction. Over the years, not only did I learn what worked for our family, and subsequently what didn't, but I also learned that most people didn't know what worked for us. How could they know when I was spending so much blood, sweat, and tears just to learn myself? Accepting the fact that we were a minority as it related to family structure was refreshingly liberating. The most difficult times for me were the ones where, for a moment, I forgot that we weren't a "normal" family, where we had just partaken in some regular event without incident only to have an incident hit me in the face like a sledgehammer. I'd usually wind up more frustrated with myself for losing touch with reality than I would with anyone or anything else.

Xavian was also different. Life skills like wiping himself, getting dressed, and eating in a tidy, pleasant way had to evolve over a long period of time. Such things couldn't be forced. They required repetition and habit, and since his behavior placed such a limit on the amount of occupational therapy he could receive, these skills were taught on a daily basis at home by Cassie and myself and at school by teachers and specialists. It took a lot of energy to fight the battles that needed to be fought, and we were constantly drained of that energy. We were invariably fatigued and weary.

Xavian learned a modified way of dressing himself and would gladly do so with a bit of nudging, but we had to nudge our typical kids as well. First, we communicated to him verbally that it was time to get dressed. Then we laid his underwear flat, face-up on the floor. We did the same for his pants or shorts. Once he put those pieces of clothing on, we laid his shirt flat, face-down on the floor. He would put his left arm in first, using his right arm to pull lefty through the hole, followed by his head and right arm. So many times it would have been easier and quicker just to put his clothes on for him, but it was in his best interest to repeat the steps of getting dressed as many times as possible. Confidence gleamed in his eyes every time he dressed himself. He wasn't doing back flips, but I could sense the satisfaction it brought him. It was an important thing that most of us take for granted. Wiping himself after using the potty was a much more delicate process that took much longer to gain momentum with, but one in which confidence and repetition were again critical.

Despite the utter hell Xavian's immune system had gone through as an infant, he rarely got sick over the years. When he did get sick, it was a fiasco. Xavian's unique, modified style of communication made it difficult to understand exactly what he was experiencing. He usually referred to nausea as aching. It took a long time, but once we figured that out, it was easier to assess those types of situations. Before we got to that point, it was quite problematic. As it is with a lot of kids, nausea was troubling and scary to Xavian, and left him feeling like it would never subside. He would constantly ask when he would feel better. It was heartbreaking. I empathized with him so deeply because I, too, hate the feeling of nausea.

When Xavian was nauseated, instead of letting his body make the decision on whether or not to expel unwanted matter from his stomach, he would make himself vomit by sticking his finger down his throat when he thought we weren't looking. We have no idea where he learned that. I suppose it's just one of those natural human tendencies we're all born with. The problem that arose, obviously, is that he put himself in danger of becoming dehydrated and malnourished. To add to that, he couldn't keep the anti-nausea medication down long enough for it to act, so he stayed nauseated as part of a vicious cycle. The most difficult and dangerous issue we dealt with in that self-induced vomiting cycle was the fact that he couldn't keep his daily medications down. These medications were vital, as they played a major role in keeping his behavior and OCD in check and helped him focus. When his body was absent of these medications, things unraveled fast. It was just another puzzle that Cassie and I had to figure out.

In this age of technology, console games, and handheld devices, Xavian went outside and played in the dirt. It was in a much different way than I did as a kid, but in the dirt nonetheless. He examined shadows cast by the sun for hours. I have always been thankful that his desire for entertainment was often so simple. Don't get me wrong, he spent his share of time on the iPad, but it wasn't always his preference.

We've had many glorious moments over the years. Small triumphs got us through many days, but like a violent thunderstorm speeding toward us from the west, blocking the warm sunlight, triumphs could quickly turn to stress, often without cause. The times that followed were frustrating and taxing, sometimes gut-wrenching, and always carried at least a touch of helplessness. We knew Xavian was frustrated. We had suspected for some time, based on various comments he would make, that he knew he was different than other kids. Then, one day, he asked me directly about it, and I'll never forget the conversation.

"Am I different from other kids?" Xavian started curiously. My heart immediately began crumbling under its own weight. I knew where the conversation was going.

"Everyone is different. Every person on Earth is different from every other person. I am unique and you are unique, and because of that we are fascinating creatures," I responded nervously, knowing I had gone way too far off into the cosmos with my response.

"Why do I have to have a buddy with me all day at school?"

"They are with you to help you get through your day, you know, when things get difficult and what not," I said, anxious as I dug for wisdom and a more concrete response. "Would you like to try to go to class without a buddy, like the other kids do?"

He paused for a minute. "No," he said as he fixated on the dry ground below.

"If you want to try it, we can talk to your teacher and give it a try."

"I don't want to. I'm done talking about this," he said, turning quiet and thoughtful. He was done with the conversation, so we went on about our day.

He may not have thought about it anymore, but I most certainly did. It was a short conversation, but a telling one that painfully bored into my emotions. Xavian had become more aware than anyone around him had realized. On paper, he shouldn't have, but for a boy who had done nothing but defy the odds since he was born, reality told a much different story. He was deeply contemplative.

Curious, concerned, fascinated, maybe even a little excited, I saw Xavian going to class without a buddy as a possibility, whereas prior to that conversation, it wasn't on my radar at all. After that, the seed was most definitely planted in my mind.

I'd spent my entire life wanting to be unique and different, only to have people around me constantly compare me to others, leaving me feeling stripped of every ounce of individuality. Now my son, possibly the most unique individual I had ever met, gave me a glimpse into a reality where he may not have cared at all about his individuality, concerning himself more with blending in with his typical classmates. This is life's Chuck Norris Roundhouse Kick to the Face in the form of irony.

Xavian and I are very similar in how much time we spend sitting still in contemplation. I can't speak to exactly where his mind goes, but I know the cogs are turning. Our personalities are much different, however, and while I prefer spending massive amounts of time alone, he prefers to always have someone by his side. I believe his codependence was birthed out of his need for assistance with his physical limitations, but mostly due to his emotional insecurities, which are a result of the emotional trauma he's experienced in his life.

It's been very difficult for me to pinpoint how Xavian feels about his individuality. He knew he was different, and I got the sense he would have loved to fall in line with everyone else, but he most definitely found safety in his codependence. Still, I encouraged him to not fear spending time alone or doing things independently. I wanted him to understand that I believed he could do anything he put his mind to, like going to class without a buddy. I constantly expressed that to him, sometimes to his frustration, at which point I promptly dropped the matter or changed the subject. My mind lives in the future, usually at the expense of the present, and looking ahead, seeing various things that would serve him well later in life was one thing I gladly and naturally gifted him.

I've never looked at my child, who wasn't able to do all the things typical kids could do, and said, "It's alright, I have two others who can do those things." Instead, I hurt for him, especially when he wanted to do certain things, but couldn't. I've tried desperately to make sense of it throughout the years. I've fought back the guilt and the resentment like the plague. I've always felt the urge and the desire to fight for him, and I have fought for him, every day. I can't imagine a life where I wasn't fighting for him.

VERSUS SCHOOL

I f you had walked into our home during the Fall of 2019 on a weekday after school, you would have thought we were in the middle of an all-out domestic brawl. There was yelling, kicking, screaming, objects being thrown, chairs being knocked over, walls being damaged, and doors being slammed. This wasn't Matt versus Cassie or Larkin versus Dante. No. Instead, it was Xavian versus school, more specifically homework, also known as the immovable object versus the unstoppable force. At the end of the day, only Cassie's patience and cool-headedness in times of chaos could have resulted in a folder with a parent's signature denoting *said homework* had been completed. Xavian struggled to express his desire to not do homework. In fact, it seemed to enrage him. This resulted in major meltdowns that went from zero to sixty in a matter of milliseconds. The late afternoon was always a challenging time in our household. It was a period when Cassie and I were both exhausted, and in no condition to partake in a brawl.

Naturally, school was always a challenge for Xavian. His circumstance was so unique. He was a highly introspective kid who asked the most intelligent questions—questions which most kids had probably never pondered, and he sometimes came across as a smart, perhaps normal kid, especially to people who didn't know him well. Xavian was anything but normal though. Schools didn't offer a curriculum for kids like Xavian because there were no kids like Xavian. Our only option was an Individualized Education Program (IEP). Successfully implementing his IEP required every single teacher, paraprofessional, and specialist who worked with him to play a very specific, important role in order to provide an acutely targeted and effective education for him.

IEPs aren't just simple documented plans, rather they're highly individualized maps that embody instructions, support, and services, created to meet a student's specific needs. Each IEP is designed to meet those needs with the goal of helping them progress and thrive in school. As a requirement, IEPs are available to students with disabilities in public and charter schools, and are covered by the Individuals with Disabilities Education Act (IDEA). This federal law guarantees all children with disabilities access to a free and appropriate public education.

Parents and Guardians must help build the IEP and ensure their student is getting the services they need. This is done by making sure very specific language is included in the IEP. For example, if your student needs services which help with dyslexia, the IEP should contain specific language stating that need. Schools and education systems aren't required to provide services for that which is not documented as part of the IEP, and as with anything else, loopholes do exist.

Some parents and guardians have experienced nightmarish situations with regard to their student's IEP. Some school systems simply struggle to provide appropriate resources, while others have hired people who just don't care or have ulterior motives. There are some school systems that have more important things on their minds, like football. It can turn into quite a song and dance. I recommend enlisting the services of a special needs lawyer or someone else highly educated on the subject who is willing to help. Regardless of the situation, it's best to do your homework and come prepared.

Fortunately, we didn't have dramatic experiences with regard to Xavian's IEP. Cassie did her homework and we always went in as a team. There were certainly adjustments to be made along the way with a child who was constantly changing, but we found the teachers and specialists accommodating and felt like they had our best interest at heart.

Even though an IEP isn't just a written plan, the written plan is a major piece of the puzzle, as it helps with setting goals and tracking progress. The high-level outline of Xavian's written plan looked something like the following:

- Strengths of the student

- Parental concerns for enhancing the education

- Student preferences and/or interests

- Results of the most recent evaluations

- The academic, developmental, and functional needs of the student

- Special instructional factors

- Transportation

- Nonacademic and extracurricular activities

- Method/frequency for reporting progress of attaining goals to parents

- Within each area (reading, math, language, and executive functioning/organization), the following sections are measured and documented:

    - Present level of academic achievement and functional performance

    - Measurable annual goal (related to meeting the student's needs)

- Date of mastery of annual goal

- Type(s) of evaluation for annual goal

- Benchmarks

Comprehensive and unique details related to how Xavian needed to receive an education were documented within these high-level sections. If at any point during a school year we, as parents and guardians of Xavian, felt that the plan was off course, we had the right, by law, to schedule a meeting with the teachers and specialists to adjust his IEP.

Things didn't always go as planned. If Xavian was having a difficult day at school in his inclusion class, which is a class where general educators and special educators work together to meet the needs of all students, then he would be pulled out and his special educator would work with him in their classroom. Agility and flexibility were key, but structure was king. The educators at Hall-Kent Elementary School prioritized special education in a way that let kids with special needs to go to class like any other kid, so as much as their circumstances allowed. Surrounding a kid who had special needs with plenty of structure was necessary and highly beneficial. This played well across the entire scope of Xavian's IEP.

We lived down the street from our kids' elementary school, only a short minute or two walk away. While our other kids were walking to school by themselves by third grade, Xavian walked with us through fifth grade, his entire tenure at the elementary school. His impulsivity and decision making were simply too unpredictable. Even if we could have figured out a way for him to walk by himself, his codependence would have no part of it. He wanted Cassie or myself, usually both of us, as well as our dog, to walk him to school every day. At the end of the day, while other kids were walking home or to the nearby park by themselves, we walked to school and picked Xavian up in the back, where kids in the lower grades were dismissed. While it would have been a golden opportunity for us to give him more independence, it was simply too risky.

Overall, school was a good thing for Xavian. It allowed him to be around typical kids, as well as kids with special needs. All the kids knew him, and by fifth grade, most of them were mature and aware enough to understand that he was much different than they were. They were taught to embrace his differences and to be part of Xavian's support system. He was also afforded the opportunity to interact with, assist with, and learn more about kids who had special needs more intense or restrictive than his own. He expressed concern for those students, showed a little hesitancy at times, and shared his unique perspective on their situations. That experience was worth its weight in gold. School forced a level of independence that was much more difficult to provide for him at home, and his speech and fine motor skills improved drastically. Equally as important, school provided a time for Cassie to breathe and get the respite she desperately needed, although some days the seven-hour period felt more like a brief intermission at best.

THE BARRIER

*T*ears raged down our faces like four waterfalls leaping off a crag, crashing down a thousand feet into the valley below. Cassie and I sat in chairs facing one another, separated by a thick glass divider. We were surrounded by space, just endless, empty space. The floor beneath us was a dark, winding creek continuously fed by our tears. The divider which separated us spanned infinitely up, down, left, and right. It looked unbreachable. A billion stars and galaxies were painted beautifully in the black sky above, and faintly echoed on the dark, wet floor below. The darkness swallowed our light, leaving only subdued traces of detail, mostly of our faces.

If not for the luminescence drizzling down from the cosmos above, there would have been only dark. The air was frigid and each breath yielded spirited clouds of vapor that lasted only an instant. Our anticipative hearts eagerly conversed as they beat rapidly. The emotion *from the heavens above had fallen softly, and it could only be shared between us, for our souls were the only ones allowed into the depths to understand its purpose. No other keys were issued. We were alone, away from our children, away from everyone, in silence, sharing tears, sharing feelings, floundering in exhaustion, uttering not a single word.*

As a sharp, debilitating wedge constantly ripped the bond between us, an unimaginably powerful magnetism brought us back together over and over again. Logically, with adequate force, angle, and commitment, resentment should have blasted intimacy out of existence, but it was not to be. We looked for ways around the divide which separated us, but there were no chinks in this armor. Perplexed and defeated, we pressed our hands against the glass, perhaps to admit defeat, as we had fought the good fight. All that was left to do was lean in toward one another. As our nervous hands approached the glass, our heads wilted and our eyelids grew heavy.

This was no ordinary glass though. No submission would be necessary. In fact, there was no glass at all. It was only water, perfectly pure and carelessly clear. The great unbreachable divide which had inoculated us with feelings of helplessness, hopelessness, and defeat was merely an aquatic illusion. Feelings of subjugation were promptly exchanged for a strong sense of triumph. That which previously seemed to exist in a solid, impenetrable state, proved fluid and passable. This revelation brought instant joy to our souls, and our eyes intensified in amazement. The only action which remained was simple—go to her. So, I did.

As I gingerly breached the divide, which was no divide at all, I found it was even more of an illusion than we had realized. It was only energy—a thick, dense energy, existing in space-time and bending everything around it, like gravity or atmosphere. Passing through this energy felt like a magical massage to my soul. Once I pushed through the divergence, Cassie and I embraced, then turned into light and became one with the energy.

GOODBYE MEMPHIS

The year 2001 was a time of utter chaos in my life. I felt lost, scared, and unable to see much of a future, which for someone who lives in the future as I do, was quite enervating. There were also the terrorist attacks in New York, which left so many of us feeling angry and anxious. I didn't care too much for my job, or work at all for that matter. I was living a wild night life with no direction, very few real friends, and absolutely no sense of purpose whatsoever.

A few years removed from college, adult life wasn't going the way I had hoped. I was army-crawling out of one particularly topsy-turvy relationship and suffocating from regret brought on by several other failed relationships with women. My sister had told me a few years earlier that I was going to meet someone, like a soul mate, when I least expected it. I blew off that nugget of wisdom as a gesture of comfort. My recent experience had convinced me otherwise. Like Morpheus from the movie *The Matrix* said though, "Fate, it seems, is not without a sense of irony."

One year later, at the age of 26, fate, or perhaps irony, walked right into the living room of my friend's home as I stood curiously in the middle of a long, dark hallway anticipating its arrival—or should I say, *her* arrival. As nervous sweat cooled my neck, my heart slowed to a crawl. I'm certain I stopped breathing for a minute or two.

"You're not breathing. Just breathe," I told myself.

Everything went silent. Then she walked in. The highly anticipated arrival, by a few friends and myself, of a girl named Cassie was upon us. She was in the building. Undoubtedly, this was a goddess sent down from Heaven to save me from my wretched life on Earth. She was tall, thin, and beautiful with a bob hairstyle. I loved everything about her. Her enthusiasm. The way she walked. The way she held herself. She was very smooth and relaxed. The way she responded to me when we were chatting, and how she focused on me as if I actually mattered. It wasn't necessarily what either of us said. She was just present. She was remarkable. I was allowed to be myself with her. There was a magnetizing energy there.

In my amazement, one major detail was lost. She was a blonde. Girls with blonde hair never seemed to like me, and I had never dated one. They seemed like rare creatures who may not have really existed. Internally, I had always concluded that higher-quality guys, who were taller or had better bodies or who possessed greater amounts of charisma, were the ones who got the blondes, not socially awkward, mysterious guys like me. This illogical conclusion, that hair color somehow determined the level of guy a girl would talk to, was flawed at best, but insecurity can manifest itself in the most peculiar ways and produce such quirky thought patterns.

"You must be Cassie," I said with confidence in my voice.

"Yep," she replied with the most vibrant smile I'd ever seen.

There was one problem. She was taken. By that, I mean she had a boyfriend who was a mutual friend of ours. That didn't stop me from being her friend though. "Oh well," I thought, as I talked myself down from a what-if place. "Maybe we can be friends and I'll just have a really beautiful friend. Nothing wrong with that."

That night, a group of us went out for dinner and a movie, and honestly, in my heart at least, I felt like I was on a date with her. We randomly sat right next to one another during the movie. The movie was *Signs*, which is a suspense film. Throughout the night, our hearts seemed to race in synchronicity. Some connections are perfectly undeniable. When one's desire for another is reciprocated by the other person, the doors to the prison cell of their hearts slowly slide open and all that raging energy is freed. It's an unrivaled feeling.

Over the next year, she and I would chat occasionally. I would share my pain through difficult times and she would listen and be a supportive friend. Although we lost touch for a few years, I would think about her sometimes, but there were other girls and I was young, wild, and extremely unsettled. It's probably a good thing we lost touch for a moment, so that I could move past some unhealthy things in my life.

In the Fall of 2004, while I was driving to Memphis to see a girl who I had long since given up on, and with whom I was just going through the motions until someone better came along, I received a call on my cell phone. It was Cassie. She informed me she was single and I was immediately overjoyed. Not only had a beautiful friend-girl called me, but I had my way out of that other mess. The Memphis trips ended that weekend and the Birmingham trips began the next.

"GOODBYE MEMPHIS!" I shouted out the truck window enthusiastically, while traveling seventy miles per hour, southbound on Interstate 55 in Tennessee. Did I mention I was young, wild, and unsettled? The next adventure was about to begin and I had no plans to ever return to Memphis. I slammed that chapter shut.

Little did I know, this was the woman I would walk through hell with and come out the other side more in love with than when we started. If I had to relive our story, facing childhood cancer and every other major challenge we've had together in this life a hundred more times, I would still choose her every time. Intentionality, commitment, respect, and selflessness is what has made us work. When those ingredients were present, we hummed like an engine. When they weren't, we struggled like my Ram into the repair bay on our first trip to Birmingham. Sure, love plays a major role as well, but it takes more than love for a marriage to work. Throughout our journey with childhood cancer and special needs, there were many times I would have surely given up if not for her. I'm infinitely grateful for having such an amazing partner.

WEDGES, CREVICES, AND EMPTY TANKS

As parents of a child with special needs, we have to be flexible. We have to expect there to be a blockade at every turn and be willing to make the necessary adjustments in order for our child's needs to be met. There is no time for getting comfortable. Comfort is short-lived and craving it is almost unfair to ourselves. When you have a child with special needs, it's you, your child, and walls everywhere. Some of these walls are so short you can simply hop over them in stride, while others are tall and must be scaled. The tall ones cause anxiety, stress, and present innate dangers. It's like navigating life inside a maze. Everyone else, unless they are making some very specific and profound impact in your life, often cannot receive your attention in an effective way or in any realistic capacity. I like to think of it as a formula of availability.

Urgency + Priority - Energy = Availability.

Being someone who, most of the time, cannot communicate my thoughts and feelings effectively or accurately, this formula has proven problematic as I have struggled mightily at times to explain to people why I disappear mentally and emotionally for long periods of time. People generally don't understand this type of behavior because it's rare and unusual. I've often used the analogy that when my stress cup fills up, there is simply no room for more stress, so things that cause stress can't be added to the cup. It causes an overflow, and overflows are *messy*, so I must withdraw to avoid torpefying messes. Try pouring coffee into a cup which is already full sometime. There's a requirement for the level to decrease before pouring more coffee. It's such a rudimentary concept, yet everyone seems to struggle with it. Sometimes it takes patience, but I've found that people don't always have patience, especially as it relates to other people. The coffee represents stress, and nobody has to take on any more stress than is naturally given to them.

Cassie and I took mental breaks when our kids were in school. It provided us with long periods of rest, five days a week, nine months a year. There were even moments of relaxation on weekends and holidays. However, as the parents of a child with special needs, we *never* truly rested. Something in our brain remained in the "on" position when normally it should have shut off for a bit. There's probably science to describe that phenomenon, but I haven't researched it, probably because I don't need to. I lived it every day and I felt it strongly. Because of that, respite, a word we hear thrown around so often, is sort of an illusion. Yes, it's there. Yes, there are times when we get breaks, but that part of the brain which never shuts off also doesn't allow respite to incite the feelings everyone expects it to. I fully understand the reason behind respite, and I'm thankful for the amazing organizations and people who provide it to us, but I also strongly feel the reality or illusion of it in my mind.

As it relates to marriage, trauma is a jackhammer, and what is left behind is made up of wedges, crevices, and empty tanks. Trauma comes in first and relentlessly attempts to demolish the foundation upon which the marriage is built and the individuality of both members of that bond. The impact can be abrupt or it can take place over a period of time, often in waves. What remains of a once-pristine building standing tall over an uncluttered lot is now a damaged, struggling structure atop a fragmented foundation where the grass has turned to dirt and the weeds are creeping their way through the chain-linked fence, consuming the very essence of the land.

As our energy reserves were depleted daily, and we reached in deeper and deeper for just a droplet of something to get us through, Cassie and I grew weary. When there's no energy left at all, there's no energy left for one another. As wedges were vehemently pounded into those crevices which remained from the trauma, we fought with all we had to drive them out, filling the rifts with the only things we had—commitment, love, and common ground.

Cassie and I needed each other's support. We'd grown so accustomed to it. A few years after Xavian's Hemispherectomy surgery, I realized I wasn't providing the level of support she needed. Sure, I was struggling in my own right, but there were two of us and she needed more support than she was getting from me. I was thankful to be awoken to that fact and I began steadily making adjustments. In the same breath, I needed more support as well. It was just a struggle all around, and stress does something to a person. It takes you to places you don't want to go.

Sometimes we can't breathe and we just need someone next to us to put the oxygen mask on and hold it there while we struggle to catch our breath as tears of panic pour out of both eyes. It feels like drowning and it's a reality we cannot escape. Even couples who have kids with no special needs or no kids at all still need support. That's how fundamental it is to a committed relationship. Life finds a way to make vulnerability and dependence necessary. The reasons may differ, but the need still exists. Trials in life are relative and equal opportunity. It's just another reason we shouldn't compare our lives to the lives of others.

Marriage requires daily renewal, and the couples who are able to recognize this necessity and put it into practice are the ones who are most likely to make it through the storm together. In football, the defensive back has possibly the toughest position. They have to line up one-on-one with the nearly impossible job of stopping blazing fast, quick-footed, shifty wide receivers (most of whom are well over six feet tall), and while the wide receivers know where they are running to—the defensive back does not. Sure, there is sometimes safety help over the top, but I'm making a point. That point is, in marriage, if there's an argument or a disappointment or any type failed expectation, much like when a defensive back gets beat on a pass to a wide receiver, the ones who find the most success are the ones who can move past the last play, or in the case of marriage the last failed expectation or argument. It requires a short memory.

When I think of two people connected in marriage, I think of a straight path with both people walking it together, trajectories intertwining but rarely, if ever, equidistant to the path or to one another. At times, both people are moving away from one another. Other times, they are moving toward one another. This is what makes marriage challenging and it's why controlling people have a hard time staying married. It's incredibly difficult to control someone who is moving away and then back again. It creates unwarranted friction and resentment, and I've seen it happen so many times. The most successful couples are the ones who can hold on loosely to one another when they come together, and not stray too far in opposite directions when they are moving away. People who are controlling, grip far too tightly, breaking the fragile bond of marriage. It's not natural.

I've learned through the giving and receiving of support with Cassie that it has to be done with genuineness. Sure, we can provide x, y, or z to our partner out of duty, but it doesn't necessarily elevate the relationship toward its pinnacle. When support and love are given with a true heart, they are also received in that same manner.

Internally, I got to a point where I refused to let it count if I didn't provide for Cassie with a true heart, even though outwardly-focused stress tried to tell a different story. My marriage was the highest priority in my life, as far as interpersonal relationships are concerned. My kids, parents, grandparents, siblings, aunts, uncles, cousins, and friends were just *not* as important. Parents with kids still living at home will certainly have to prioritize their kids just under their spouse because they are still under their care. I have to make adjustments. If pulling away from other relationships in order to strengthen and maintain a loving, healthy relationship with my wife through the everyday trials of caring for a child with special needs is what it takes, then I have to do that. I'm not responsible for any relationship with anyone other than those who walk closely with me on a daily basis. It seems like a simple formula, but you'd be amazed at how often these priorities become misplaced in peoples' lives.

I grew to learn that I needed to be closer to Cassie, both physically in support of her and metaphorically. If she was being spit on, then I should be spit on too. But the balance between my own limitations and fears, and providing Cassie with unbridled support, was one of my most formidable foes, and one that I never surrendered to. On paper, our marriage should have crumbled. It should have imploded due to the pressures brought on by the depths to which it was taken, but somehow it didn't. There were many occasions where I didn't think our marriage could keep going as it ran on fumes. It seemed the constant pounding we were taking would cause us to crumble beneath the ruins of our own selves. After all, in our case, the person who was there to lift, support, and energize you was, themself, crumbling. Sure, we both had supportive friends, but comparing the support a friend can provide with the support a significant other should is comparing apples with oranges.

I can only speculate that common values, faith, commitment, and ultimately grace saved our marriage. I didn't mention love, because of course I love my wife. Love alone does not save marriages, even though it's a critical ingredient. The only explanation I have for how we had enough strength to carry the immense weight placed upon our marriage throughout our journey is that something supernatural or spiritual provided for us.

Whenever both people in a marriage are stressed, everything becomes magnified and attraction can easily turn to repulsion through magnetic reversal, or "flip" in scientific terms. Most, if not all, of our struggles stemmed from the fact that caring for Xavian required massive amounts of energy collectively and individually, especially when he was home for extended periods like summer break or holidays. Our energy is our essence. Once it's depleted, there is only survival. Undoubtedly, a willingness to protect your spouse's energy like the precious gem it is can only help a marriage succeed. With kids, the formula for energy becomes much more complex, as a major part of parenting is understanding the energy of your kids and helping them best manage it within themselves and the confines of the family unit. It's astoundingly difficult.

There were days where I sincerely thought I was losing my mind. Those were the days where I didn't share my feelings with Cassie, out of fear that she didn't have the energy to manage it, as I knew she was struggling as much, if not more than I was at the time. Sometimes, managing your spouse's energy is less about what they are already struggling with and more about how you are handling your energy in relation to that. You have to be careful though, as resentment can sneak in and really muck things up. You have to find the tipping point that sits perfectly between revealing too much of your feelings and too little. I was never good at finding that balance, often revealing too little.

When you are required to give so much of yourself to something in your life, like a child with special needs, everything else is at risk of suffering. This includes relationships, work, and health, among other things. It's not a conscious decision you make, where you lay your energy out on a table in front of you and divvy up the amount to suit your desires. With marriage, it's twice as hard because there are two people with different energetic needs, who are both dealing with challenges, and both parents are giving it their best. There are going to be moments when things try to unravel. Trying to keep it all from unwinding is going to get ugly. Suppressed feelings are going to emerge. Jealousy could escape. There are a lot of things that could go really badly if you run out of fight.

In the 1990s, the Chicago Bulls won an unprecedented six championships in eight years. During the six championship seasons, they faced only two game sevens in best of seven series. During their sixth and final championship run in 1998, they faced a game seven in the Eastern Conference Finals against an Indiana Pacers team that gave them a lot of trouble. Before that game, Phil Jackson, "The Zen Master," told his team, "You can lose. You have to face the possibility that you can lose a game like this." What The Zen Master was trying to get his team to understand was they needed to prepare themselves mentally to not stop fighting until that final buzzer sounded, and when it did, if they had lost, then there was no shame in that.

Marriage is the same way. You can lose. That possibility does exist. There's no absolute guarantee that your marriage, or my marriage, or anyone's marriage will stand the test of time and all the stress life is going to throw at it. There are a million different ways a marriage can fail. Anyone getting married should think about that, so they can understand that marriage is not free. It should be treated less like a lottery ticket and more like hard-earned money. You gain a lot from marriage, but you have to pay for it in a plethora of uncomfortable ways. At the end of the day, it's about you being able to say that you fought until you were lifeless and there was nothing left in the tank. If you did all you could, then there's absolutely nothing to be ashamed of if it fails. In fact, you should be proud that you went down fighting. There is honor in that.

When you love someone, there's a particular feeling that claws, grasps, and rapes. It's the one where your significant other is hurting and there's nothing you can do to stop it. Whether it be from a migraine headache or from a child of whom the word explosive somehow doesn't quite get the point across. I've often heard that a person cannot be held responsible for the happiness of another, but I believe a good husband does accept the responsibility for his significant other's happiness. Not taking responsibility may play well in short-term, non-romantic relationships, but in marriage it leads to aloofness, blame, a lack of accountability, and almost always heartfelt pain followed by divorce. In some cases, one spouse may not be able to bring happiness to their significant other, but there should be a determination, a will, and a focus to do everything in their power to bring delight to their beloved.

ALONE IN TIME

As someone who needs a lot of alone time to recharge my battery and map out life courses, I've really struggled at times. I've been blessed for the past seven years of my twenty-plus career as a software developer to work remotely, where I can work in solitude and receive the alone time I need. I've tried my best to make myself available for assistance to Cassie with clinic visits and other Xavian-related things, and I've been blessed to be with companies where the people in charge understood the demands we've faced on a daily basis.

My career, in a sense, has been taken hostage by those demands though. By that I mean I am severely limited in the jobs I can take, as not all companies are so sympathetic. There's also the financial demand it has placed on us. Luckily, I've been fortunate to have only had three jobs since I graduated college in 1999 and perhaps even more lucky to have been placed with people who understand that family is more important than money. My job has always sort of been a respite for me, and I've almost always enjoyed the work, but when it was stressful, life was stressful, regardless of what was happening at home. A job should never come before family, and my only regret with respect to my career are those times when I allowed it to.

There's no doubt I lost who I was somewhere along the way during this journey. The beautiful thing is, through a series of very distinct and serendipitous events, that former shell I wore, which had been created and molded for so long by so many people, broke away. I began to find someone else beneath it—the real me. This phenomenon allowed me to put things into perspective, to see life not through the lens of some set of instilled values painted on by someone else's selfish desires, traditions, or principles, but rather through a window into reality and an existence where I can unapologetically be who I was created to be. I'm a sensitive intuitive who now understands that I don't have to put myself in harm's way for empty achievement. I don't have to be successful in my career. Success in my career is very low on my list. I don't have to have certain friends or live in certain places. Someone else can keep up with the Joneses. I absolutely do not care one ounce what other people are doing. I literally don't have to do anything or be anyone except for who I was created to be. If this falls outside the expectations for anyone who knows me, so be it.

My forties have been the most challenging, darkest times of my life, but they've also been the most liberating, joyful times. It's amazing how walking through darkness can help you find light. I feel like a lot of things have aligned recently in my universe. I don't think that is a coincidence. In fact, I think the struggles have not only helped me find my true core, but have pointed me toward my destiny and moved me much closer to finding my purpose. In fact, if not for one extremely painful, but powerful life situation completely unrelated to our journey with Xavian, I would not have written this book.

If you asked me if I would go through the debilitating pain of that situation again if it was the only way I would be able to write this book, the answer would be an *emphatic* "YES!" We have to learn to see pain for what it is, a compass, offering direction, guiding us in our journey. The purpose of pain is not for us to be hurt, but for us to listen. It's a code—a means of communication. Whether that comes from our brain, from God, from the universe, or from another version of ourselves in another dimension, I think we should listen. Sometimes that compass sends us straight through the heart of our greatest fears, and if we aren't willing to blast through that with discomfort, tears, anxiety, and achy stomachs, then we will miss out on the greatest things life has to offer. We must communicate with pain by first listening. We must ask ourselves:

"What is it telling me?"

"Why is it telling me this?"

"What should I do, if anything?"

"When should I take this action?"

We must also celebrate the clear skies because they come and go so quickly, and our perception of time is abstract and extremely fragile. It seems we lose it too quickly. It slips away from us, and if we're not paying attention, we're left with nothing but consequences and memories. If we are paying attention, we're left with a gift.

One lesson I learned is I didn't have to put my life on hold because of the bloody, internal, emotional war I was in with myself over our situation with Xavian. I found that the closer we got to our version of normal, the better off we were. It's alright to mourn and grieve that which has been lost, but it doesn't have to leave us with permanent paralysis. At times, we are going to ball up into the fetal position, we are going to cry uncontrollably, and we're not going to feel like doing anything, and that's alright. Take that time and use it to heal, and never accept anyone's attempt to interrupt your healing. There's not a more unempathetic action than to trespass into the property of someone's soul when they are in the process of healing. We can be damaged, hurt, and broken, but that doesn't mean we're useless. I've found that people do the most amazing things while they're broken.

SLEEPING CHILD

Y ou won't find another child who transitioned from chaos to peace as quickly as Xavian did. When fatigue would set in at the end of each day, and his body and mind were exhausted from the turmoil thrown his way by a disadvantageous life, there was no fighting sleep like other kids often did. It was bedtime and his expectation was that the sound machine was turned up to the highest volume, the fan turned to the highest setting, every light in the room turned off, and the door shut. Once those boxes were checked, Xavian was in dreamland. This unique behavior hasn't changed over the years. It's a touch of much needed calm after the storm. Our edgy, codependent, fiery little guy slept peacefully—an atypical, but amazing phenomenon indeed.

Conversely, for me, the sudden transition of being on edge to a more relaxed state was like being in a vehicle that was going a hundred miles per hour and came to a sudden stop. It was jarring. After Xavian was tucked in, with his trundle bed pulled out, sheets and blankets in place, sound machine on, curtains drawn, and door closed, I breathed a slow, deep breath of relief, which was usually followed by a huge wave of emotion that swallowed me whole. I would be tossed about like sand in the ocean. In that moment, I was exhausted from fighting the good fight and overcome with gratitude, but paralyzed all the same.

Committing to a television series or movie felt too energetically expensive. Finding the energy to write seemed impossible. Trying to think just hurt too badly, and trying to talk hurt more. Playing video games always sounded fun, but that too required a certain amount of energy and commitment, which I couldn't generally muster. After a long, stressful, seemingly never-ending day with Xavian, usually Sunday, I would stand at the bar that separated our kitchen from our living area feeling helpless, unable to shed a tear, when I really needed a river of tears to wash away the stress and send it swiftly on its way. I felt like a boxer who had just finished a twelve-round fight.

That anticipated respite, which I desired throughout the day, most often turned into a wrestling match with anxiety at night—a wrestling match I rarely won. Reflection upon the mistakes I had made during the day sent my mind into a tailspin. It was debilitating. No one was harder on me than me. Thoughts of tomorrow and the inadequacy I felt as a parent consumed my confidence and left me defeated. No matter how elegant the game plan was, the execution never seemed to work quite right.

"Am I even equipped to guide him where he needs to go?" I often asked myself at night while he was sleeping. "How can I find success in this as a parent? How can he be successful in his journey?"

The answers never came. The puzzle was too complex. There were too many pieces to place.

My parental shortcomings left me feeling ill-equipped to overcome such a fierce battle. Emotional paralysis and hopelessness were relentless in their attacks. A storm was upon us and there was nowhere to run, nowhere to hide, not enough energy to obtain the needed information, and not enough time to change. Alcohol, television, reading, meditation, and prayer sometimes served as effective, temporary escapes, but God remained patiently silent and the universe seemed so—physical.

I always reflected on my fatherhood and felt like I could have done better. I was never proud of what I remembered. Looking ahead always left me feeling like I could never do enough. I was never satisfied with what I imagined. Parenting is as difficult as it is unforgiving. Maybe that's the way it's supposed to be.

ADOLESCENCE, MEET PANDEMIC

A s Xavian entered adolescence, the intensity of his behavioral challenges intensified greatly. What once consisted of spitting and clenching of his fist or throwing himself to the ground, morphed into destruction of property, self-harm, aggression toward others, verbal abuse, and still—spitting. Only, by that time, the spitting had turned from what appeared more like a means of self-regulation into an attempt to humiliate whomever the target of his aggression was. Maybe it was a statement of defiance more than anything. Whatever it was, it was usually targeted at Cassie or myself.

While many kids struggled with just one or two behavioral and emotional disorders, Xavian was struggling with many. Attention deficit hyperactivity disorder (ADHD), oppositional defiant disorder (ODD), autism spectrum disorder (ASD), anxiety disorder, depression, bipolar disorder, learning disorders, and conduct disorders all presented challenges in some measurable capacity.

In my experience with him, the behavioral disorders, or behavioral struggles as I prefer to call them, had a few very distinct characteristics.

Behavioral struggles were constant. Sure, there may have been some bi-polar or other diagnosis-related aspect to the fact that the behavioral struggles didn't go away, but there always seemed to be two main ingredients—triggers and resulting behaviors. When his triggers were squeezed, just like that of a firearm, the resulting behavior was an explosion.

Behavior was sometimes inconsistent. Due to variables unbeknownst to us, once in a while, a particular trigger resulted in a different behavior than what we were accustomed to. While the trigger-behavior phenomenon remained constant, we didn't always get exactly what we expected, which made it difficult to get out in front of the resulting behavior.

Behavior was intense. The raw power of Xavian's emotions, and the extreme fluctuations from one emotion to the next, made for some fierce outbursts on a daily basis. There were days when we enjoyed moments of peace, sometimes hours, then out of nowhere, all hell would break loose and every ounce of tranquility was thrust away like dirt into a vacuum cleaner. This resulted in our confidence being temporarily flattened like memory foam. Sure, that confidence eventually shifted back into its original form, but until that happened, we struggled.

Behavioral struggles were private. They didn't always display themselves for outsiders—people outside our immediate household. We would have people over to our home and they'd only see the mildest forms of these behavioral struggles, so they probably thought, "Oh, it's not that bad. I don't know why they're making such a big deal out of it." The reality is, they'd seen the volcano lightly smoking from a distance, but hadn't been up close and felt the eruption of fury with molten lava thrust a mile into the sky.

Behavior was not always conscious. There were times when Xavian seemed out of his mind. Those were the times when he attempted self-harm the most, and inflicted harm upon us when we tried to prevent it. It felt unconscious and uncontrollable, like an Incredible Hulk scenario.

Finally, *behavioral struggles were not always forgiving.* After one of Xavian's major meltdowns, the mental and physical energy exerted in containing his and my emotions, while keeping him from hurting himself or destroying something, was so great that I'd literally be sick to my stomach afterwards. I would be left feeling mentally hopeless, emotionally defeated, and physically unwell. I couldn't always just leave the house and take a walk either, especially if I was the only parent home at the time of the meltdown. Leaving a child with special needs home alone was simply not an option. Sometimes, taking any sort of break wasn't an option. On many occasions, during the moments following a meltdown, Xavian would go right back to being codependent like nothing had ever happened. I, on the other hand, would be left drained from the toll it had just taken on me. On a day where there were multiple meltdowns, one can only imagine the despair we found ourselves in.

In March of 2020, when the Coronavirus Pandemic began its conquest, all of a sudden, everyone in the world had a new perspective from which to survey their struggles. For me as a remote employee and an introvert who required much time alone, life didn't really change that much. For Cassie, who was more extroverted, socializing wore a new mask and this new routine squeezed a bit more tightly.

As parents of a child with special needs, our biggest challenge remained the same though—our struggles were already in perspective. When normal for everyone else changed into a life lived in fear, a forced routine, and constant uncertainty, I deeply empathized with them because they were suddenly living something which much more closely resembled our daily struggle.

During this time, we continued our search for a psychiatrist who could instill, at the very least, some trace of confidence in us.

Our first meeting with our third psychiatrist in less than eighteen months took place during the Coronavirus pandemic, so we used a remote video conference. As the previous psychiatrist had done, he immediately identified errors with the regimen prescribed by the psychiatrist before him. It was already a difficult time with Xavian entering adolescence and changing a lot, but his medications just weren't right. We knew that. It's the main reason we kept changing psychiatrists. The other reason was we wanted someone who was caring, and would openly listen to us and respond to our intellect in an appropriate way. We wanted to be heard and we wanted a teammate, not a dictator—and we finally got what we wanted in Dr. Gurmendi (Dr. G).

Xavian's self-harm attempts were at an all-time high and keeping him from banging his head on a hard surface or piercing the skin on his arm with a bite became a full-time job, as these behaviors could spin up faster than a Texas tornado. When consciously present, Xavian could work through his frustrations by reacting with spitting, verbal abuse, or harmlessly biting his arm. But when impulsivity sent him into an unconscious rage, he would go into Hulk-mode and attempt to bang his head on the closest physical object that could provide feedback, whether that be something hard like the ground or a table, or something soft like a pillow or mattress. He would also try to rip the skin from his arm with his teeth. Meltdowns were sparked by all sorts of things, such as his siblings making a face at him or saying the wrong thing to him, the dog barking, someone coughing or sneezing, words not flowing out the way he expected them to, or something simply not going his way.

Dr. G provided us with an organized and methodical way to move toward something better for Xavian. Due to the speed with which his impulsivity manifested itself, there were times when it was not physically possible to reach him before an action, like banging his head, had taken place. We put as many measures as we possibly could in place, including mandating he wear a helmet when his mood was most volatile. Many of those measures meant sacrifice on our part.

We became experts on predicting when an impulsive explosion might occur, and we never stopped making adjustments, whether subtle or appreciable. We molded our routine around keeping our son safe from self-harm, willing to do whatever it took. We kept trying things and we kept failing, over and over and over, but we never gave up on him. We weren't the most organized household, or skilled at tracking and capturing behavioral trends, even though Cassie and I often discussed ways we could achieve that goal. Ultimately, I accepted the fact that it wasn't going to happen. It just wasn't "us." We had to accept being content with just surviving.

To muddy our waters even more during the 2020 pandemic, Xavian began vomiting regularly, with no fever or other symptoms, and appeared to be in discomfort anytime he swallowed. Anytime he swallowed, he would grasp the right side of his head near his ear. When we asked him if it hurt, he would get upset and say that he was embarrassed by it. He wasn't interested in discussing it. Medical professionals couldn't figure it out either. He also began complaining of a burning in his stomach.

During a time when nobody was going anywhere for fear of contracting the Coronavirus, we were visiting the pediatrician fairly often. After the first trip and two ineffective antibiotics (prescribed for an ear infection), Xavian was still hurting. Not only that, but a second trip to the pediatrician revealed he was extremely constipated. By that point, we only relied on our pediatrician for things like physicals, scheduled exams, and run-of-the-mill illnesses. Understandably, they just didn't seem confident in assessing Xavian. There were simply too many variables at play.

Our next step included a visit to the emergency room. I'm not sure if it was due to a lack of effort, or if Xavian truly was an unsolvable puzzle like I had submitted to many times before, but that trip to the emergency room proved completely useless. We received no direction whatsoever. Yet, we were still billed—a flawed system indeed. I literally could not have rolled my eyes any further into the back of my head. The great American Health System struck a chord with me, once again.

In addition to physical health challenges, Xavian continued to struggle with mental health issues as his OCD once again flared up and greatly intensified. He would try to repeat phrases and words in his mind a certain number of times. When he was unable to do so, or "couldn't get it," as he termed it, he experienced extreme anxiety, and that caused a great physical pain in his abdominal area. He also kept scratching the inside of his eye socket between his eye and the bridge of his nose until it was raw. Unfortunately, this became a major issue when he was playing outside in the sand or dirt because he couldn't use his left hand to remove the dust particles from his right hand, so he inevitably got sand or dirt in his eye, which ignited fiery meltdowns.

As had always been the case since our journey began, when answers didn't come easily and a thick fog settled down over our lives, commitment, gratitude, hope, and perhaps most inconspicuously, dignity got us through. We were most definitely running on fumes though.

We never stopped troubleshooting Xavian's symptoms, specifically the vomiting and constipation. We were finally able to see a gastroenterologist (GI doctor). He ran various tests, but could only determine that Xavian's hemiparesis was most likely to blame for his frequent constipation. Xavian was also taking two antipsychotic medications, an OCD medication, and a PRN (as needed) anxiety medication. This regimen most likely contributed to his constipation as well. Our GI doctor added a stool softener and a natural, veggie-based laxative to Xavian's regimen, and we began increasing his exercise as much as his behavior would allow. This helped us to get his constipation under control.

Once the constipation and self-harm were under control, the vomiting settled. As we put another piece of the puzzle into place, my frustration with having to figure out so much, with little help from the medical professionals who are paid to do so, grew. I was reminded during that time that no medical professional in today's American healthcare system was going to troubleshoot my child's symptoms the way Cassie and I would. They were just there as a checkbox in our troubleshooting process. I believe this is the mindset every parent going through a similar journey will have to be in.

Prior to July 2020, Xavian essentially had no useful diagnosis. Traumatic Brain Injury wasn't the trendy diagnosis we had to have for the services he needed. We knew Xavian was on the Autism Spectrum though, and we knew if we could get that officially confirmed, we would qualify for many more much-needed services. So, in late 2019 we had started the lengthy process of proving his Autistic status. After a series of interviews, testing, and a lot of waiting, in July of 2020, Xavian finally received the diagnosis which more accurately reflected reality—autism spectrum disorder (ASD). This brought his full diagnosis to left-side hemiparesis, mood disorder, attention deficit hyperactivity disorder (ADHD), obsessive compulsive disorder (OCD), and autism spectrum disorder.

In addition to receiving a concrete diagnosis during this time, Xavian reached another milestone as he began middle school. Wearing a mask to school certainly wasn't his favorite thing, but we were excited for him to be taking another step in his development and in his life.

SOCIETY

The words "Society, you're a crazy breed. I hope you're not lonely without me," rang out through my headphones as Eddie Vedder's raspy, baritone voice spoke directly into my soul. I have a love-hate relationship with society because I love people individually, but I hate them collectively. That collective, in my eyes at least, is *Society*. Society offers a unique experience for each of us. At a higher level, however, it could be the same anywhere. My disdain for society revolves around, but is not limited to, intolerance, impatience, inconsideration, and entitlement. My disgust with it comes from my personal experiences as an introverted, ethical, intuitive individual who has never really had it all that bad, especially not to the naked eye. I value the idiosyncratic, fresh views of individuals over society's unimaginative, futile stances that promote assembly line mentality. In terms of what Xavian will have to face in society, those feelings are magnified by a thousand and I feel fully justified in that.

The line between a typical child who has behavior challenges and a child who has moderate to severe special needs with a strong behavioral aspect to it is quite blurred. Some people choose to either ignore this fact, or they are far too ignorant to understand it until it is explained to them in detail, while others are so blinded by the perfect silver spoon world they've lived in their entire lives that they simply cannot see it. As a parent whose child is likely to have a meltdown anytime and anywhere, including in the middle of a grocery store, for example, I've had to create a strong boundary with regard to society, specifically with the people who are in the vicinity during such a meltdown.

That line is drawn at the expense of others' convenience. It isn't my responsibility to ensure that their shopping experience is stellar. I will conduct myself with the utmost respect, like I would if I was in someone's way of getting to a particular item on a shelf, but I will not tolerate disrespect involving my son's behavior. Simply put, I do not owe anyone an apology for my child's conduct. That doesn't mean I won't apologize to someone in a difficult moment as a show of respect or compassion. I'll most certainly offer that, but I feel absolutely no obligation to do so.

There's a difference between willingly giving something to a person and feeling mandated to do so. The same applies to anyone providing care for my son as a means of respite for Cassie and I. They know what they're signing up for, and while I can be extremely attuned to that, it doesn't mean I'm going to go around apologizing to everyone for every little behavior he exhibits. Society doesn't adjust to us. We must make our own adjustments to society.

I'm not usually a fan of hard boundaries, but with regard to the collective people and our daily dealings with special needs, they are necessary. It's up to us to determine what is acceptable and what is not and to graciously and sternly stand behind that. If you are a parent of a child with special needs, or simply struggle with society's treatment of you, I urge you to define those hard boundaries in your own life. You are not society's whipping boy, and you have as much right as anyone else to stand up and refuse to accept anything less than is fair.

In a society where nothing is free, finding services for Xavian that didn't cost an exorbitant amount of money or were covered by health insurance was no small task. It took time, which was *always* at a premium. Researching services took energy, but that energy wasn't always available. On top of that, we had to determine where to start. Even in a digital age, where communication is widespread and much more readily available, we still had to dig deep just to locate realistic options. Cassie's social networking skills helped immensely, but information pertinent to our cause was often contradictory and required considerable amounts of vetting.

During Xavian's chemotherapy treatments, hospital stays, and surgeries, we hadn't had many choices. They were made for us by our medical team. We were basically the ones who checked the last box to satisfy the legal aspects of it all. Once all of Xavian's major medical issues had been addressed by 2012, we were the baby bird being nudged out of the nest and expected to somehow fly. The mama bird medical team had moved on to the next baby bird, and wouldn't be swooping down to save us. We had to immediately learn how to navigate our new life outside of the nest while carrying a thousand pounds of emotion and fear with us. Not to mention, we were a family of five, each with a variety of individualized daily needs and care. Life doesn't have a pause button. That segue from life in a hospital, fully furnished with support all around us, to life back home, picking up the pieces, never became completely comfortable.

Experiencing Xavian's challenges at home, where we tried to build positive structure around him, always took my mind to a future place where we might not be around when he's older. Imagining his life without us poured rocket fuel onto the fire of my already extreme existential crisis. There's no more debilitating feeling than thinking of my adult child with special needs feeling scared, alone, miserable, or worse—being mistreated because Cassie and I are either deceased or not in a place where we can care for him. It's the saddest thought that has ever run rampant in my mind.

In a world full of rapists, murderers, and extremely unhealthy and uneducated people, I feared Xavian wouldn't stand a chance without us. Society would expend every ounce of energy it possessed in an attempt to chew him up, spit him out, and defeat him. Thinking on Xavian's role in society, an unmitigated helplessness clung to my conscience like gorilla glue. Knowing there are family members, friends, and even strangers who would take care of Xavian if we were gone barely took the edge off that insecurity.

There were times in our journey when we could have left Dante and Larkin with family or friends and focused on Xavian during a hospital stay, and a time or two we did, but my goal was to never shield them from that part of our journey. That goal was driven by the fact that I never wanted Dante or Larkin to question the reasons why they weren't included in the *entire* thing—the good, the bad, and the ugly. We are a family of five and we should experience things together, regardless of how atypical we are as a unit.

Caring for a sibling who has special needs is something most kids may never have the opportunity to experience. In that, a highly unique, extraordinary perspective is created and available as a blessing. I tried to sort of groom my typical kids to not just care for their brother, but to care for anyone whose abilities are compromised. Protecting my kids from their brother's life by shielding them from the difficult parts would have been nothing short of an injustice. I wanted them to understand that in life we must play the hand we are dealt and we must do it with courage. I also wanted them to understand that life is not always pretty. Watching people struggle is not pretty, but it's real all the same. I hope as they grow into adulthood their exposure to special needs yields plentiful fruit and allows them to positively affect the lives of others as society prods them unapologetically. I can't think of a better outcome from this journey for them.

Even though I feel society is a wretched, invisible, and all-encompassing entity, it doesn't mean that everyone who is part of it is bad. The concept of good and bad are such grey areas anyway. There were people, friends and strangers alike, who wanted to help us throughout our journey, but a problem arose from the fact that we didn't always know how to allow them to help. We declined help on more occasions than I care to admit, for a plethora of reasons, and sometimes for no reason whatsoever.

Often during stressful moments, like unplanned hospital stays, we refused help because it was just easier to simplify things. I like things simple. What that means during stressful times is involving fewer people. Declining help always carried a nugget of guilt for me. As a former and perhaps still borderline people-pleaser, I've never felt very comfortable letting people down, but I'm getting there. I'm eternally grateful for all the beautiful souls who have offered to step out of their comfort zone and out of their routine for the lone purpose of helping us get through a stressful situation.

MULTIVERSE

On a long summer day in 2018, as the blazing Alabama heat slowly turned my black truck into an oven, Dante and I chatted and enjoyed the comfort of modern day air conditioning. Dante had just seen the latest Spider-Man movie with some friends on the east side of town. I picked him up from the movie theater afterward and we began the twenty-minute trek home. Our conversations commonly revolved around something technical or science-fiction based. Yes, we are nerds. This particular day was no different.

"Time travel isn't possible," Dante started.

"Ohhhhh?" I responded with raised eyebrows. "What do you mean?"

"The future, present, and past are happening at the same time, so any event that is happening is happening simultaneously, so that prevents time travel from being possible."

"That's deep—and plausible. It makes sense." I nodded.

"What do you think about time travel, Daddy?" he asked curiously.

"I believe time travel is possible, but each time someone time travels, it creates a new dimension, like another universe, which is parallel to the dimension from which they came, and is fully self-contained. So if Dante, the future Dante for example, went back in time, Dante in the past would never know it because Dante from the future would be in a dimension forked from the original dimension, and void of any other Dantes. I don't think you can change the present or the future, but perhaps you can create alternate versions of them. It's pretty deep stuff, but that's my theory."

Dante sat quietly, most likely wanting to dive deeper with me into the subject, but either unwilling or unable to do so. He had presented a unique perspective on time travel, one which I hadn't previously thought of, and I think he needed some time for my theory to sink in, as I did his. I could sense the wheels turning in his head. I have to admit, my theory on time travel is a bit outlandish, if not altogether offbeat, but I've never seen it disproved. The theory doesn't fall in line with the famous movies from my era, like *Back to the Future* or *The Terminator*, but it definitely triggers creative thoughts and ignites the imagination.

I'm captivated by the concept of time in general. Time seems to have a peculiar relationship with the concept of multiple dimensions, or a multiverse, as it's commonly referred to these days. The irony of being captivated by something as incomprehensible as time is that we are bound by time. We are held captive by time. Obviously, being captivated is a different thing than being held captive, but both words are ultimately derived from the Latin word captus or "taken captive," so there is a relationship there.

I truly believe time is the key to answering questions about the universe like, "Do multiple universes, or multiverses, exist?" The problem, as I see it, is we're locked into time, thus we can't use the key, time itself, to unlock the answers we so desperately desire. Regardless of which multiverse theory you're exploring, whether it be the Infinite Universes theory, the Bubble Universes theory, the Daughter Universes theory, the Mathematical Universes theory, or any of a number of theories related to dark energy, time is a major part of it. If you're not familiar with dark energy, don't fret—it's *not* witchcraft, rather it's an astronomical phenomenon related to expansion of the universe, which is studied daily. My favorite theories are the Mirror Universe theory and String theory.

The Mirror Universe theory describes our universe as a space-time cone, which is easy to explain. Basically, space-time moves forward from a single point known as the Janus point, where the motion is chaotic. As space-time moves forward it becomes more structured and larger, like a cone. The theory goes on to predict that if you follow space-time back down the cone, you'll eventually reach the end of the cone to a point where time runs backward (in relation to time as we know it), at which point you'll enter another cone where space-time runs in the opposite direction. This theory explains that another universe may exist on the other side of our space-time cone.

String theory posits that the universe is fundamentally composed of one-dimensional strings rather than point-like particles, and what we perceive as particles are actually vibrations from the strings, each carrying a different frequency. String theory also supports the idea of other universes, which we can't see, by adding extra dimensions of spacetime and thinking of particles as miniscule vibrating loops.

Beyond these theories, which focus on how other physical universes might scientifically exist, lives something perhaps even more mysterious and perplexing—*imagination*. Most people are ever-present, always available in their immediate environment, and while they can certainly use their imagination just fine, they usually remain in, and interact with, the sensory world around them. They are the people I've always wanted to be like. Then there are people like me, who spend hours upon hours in their mind, exploring possibilities, time traveling, living out potential scenarios, solving problems, and spending time in other dimensions with people who may or may not exist. I don't need the permission of extrapolated scientific data to visit another universe. I just imagine it and I go there, outside the bounds of spacetime. It's real in my mind, so it's real to me. I could also argue it's more spiritual than anything that can be found in our physical universe.

So often, we make decisions based on time. I'm not talking about being late for something or needing to be somewhere at a specific time, rather I'm talking about taking action because we fear that we can't stay in a certain mental state beyond some time threshold. That's the power of time, and we have become in thrall to it. I've coached myself relentlessly on accepting the discomfort and not allowing time to be my ruler. For example, what if someone hurts me and I feel the need to exact revenge upon them, or simply approach them in an irritated, accusatory manner? The reason I would do that is because I don't want to carry the discomfort caused by their actions for any length of time. I might want to take my own action as soon as possible in order to relieve myself of that discomfort.

There is a relationship between comfort and time, just as there is a relationship between comfort and suffering, like I mentioned earlier. The choice one has is whether or not to give in to time or give in to discomfort. If we truly cannot transcend time in reality, then perhaps metaphorically we can transcend time by choosing to not allow it to be our lord. It's a mindset that, if practiced and improved upon, can be life changing. It has been for me thus far, but I have a million miles to go to overcome that which nips at me perpetually.

I choose to not let my mind be limited to that which I can see and touch. If I did, it wouldn't be possible for me to believe in phenomena like electricity, gravity, or galaxies, all of which we know exist. There are vast worlds, which are accessible to us through our imagination, and for some of us, we should absolutely explore those worlds, especially if in doing so, we are better able to cope with traumatic experiences, pain, or to simply achieve a better mental balance. At the time of my conversation with Dante, I didn't know yet where my mind was going to take me, as it all happened so fast, but I was about to embark on a journey within a journey—and I wasn't prepared.

IMAGINE

You can look at our journey any way you want, but for us, metaphorically at least, our son left us in 2009. He was gone. Reality had forked, like my theory on time travel. Our son didn't die, he had not passed away, his heart did not stop beating in the physical world, but he was gone and our Xavian was a different boy. If you're someone who is focused narrowly on the sensory world around you, then you could probably make a valid argument that he was the same boy, just different, but *what if* he truly was a completely different boy altogether? I believe it deserves contemplation.

Where did the other boy go? Was he really in some other place, like a parallel dimension? There's really no way to know, but it's something I've thought about often.

In my imaginative mind, I've often visited this other version of Xavian, or The Other Boy, as I've so esoterically titled this book. He's the one who didn't have a massive brain tumor rapidly grow in the right hemisphere of his head where a normal brain would sit. You might wonder where in the world I could possibly be going with such an eccentric notion. You might also wonder if I've gone mad, rambling on about parallel dimensions and alternate versions of human beings, but there's a hidden purpose and beauty in it.

I don't have any deep regret or overwhelming yearning for my son to be someone else, perfectly normal, with the same opportunity that typical kids have. If I ever did, it died the moment I met our Xavian. My son is who he is and I love him more than I could ever put into words. Of course I desire that my son, and all my kids for that matter, be given the same opportunities as any other kid. I desire for kids with special needs to have a wide range of experiences, or at least fit in and feel normal with typical kids. It breaks my heart for any family, of any race or creed, when their kids aren't given the same opportunities as other kids in society or when they are outcast. When it comes to my kids, it breaks my heart equally as much as it does for kids who are not mine.

It's all completely heartbreaking, but meeting The Other Boy was so much bigger than a trifling, vain desire for my son to be someone or something he's not. It was driven by imagination, healing, and hope, with a desire to find something deep and not easily attainable, like *gratitude*. Just pondering the possibility that, in another place or dimension, there exists a version of Xavian, this other boy, who can do everything his brother and sister can do, was incredibly intriguing and exciting, to me. That, coupled with the hope that our Xavian, who was right there with us, would continue to overcome the overwhelming odds which have been stacked against him, was very important for me to explore. It painted a picture in my mind of what Xavian was capable of and gave me creative goals to lay out for him—some realistic, others not so much, but each one taking a step in the right direction.

Imagination isn't limited to fantasies that provide no value in the real world. For those of us who can use it in a pragmatic, yet spiritual way, there are limitless possibilities. It's part of what makes me, and other intuitives like me, who we are. I'm incredibly grateful for my imagination and how it has helped me through a difficult journey, and how it has boosted my ever so fragile hope. I've spent a great deal of mental energy exploring and struggling with who Xavian is and who he would have been, along with who he can be. I think these explorations are very natural, if not mentally healthy, and healing for someone who relies heavily and constantly on intuition as a dominant cognitive processing function.

Imagination can be a tool of creativity and adventure, and

sometimes a compass in life. The key has been accepting Xavian for who he is and finding healing in that. Instead of trying to change him, I've sought ways to ignite inspiration in him and to see clearly how he can arouse inspiration in others—a task easier said than done in the midst of so much external turmoil and internal struggle, but vital nonetheless.

THE OTHER BOY

D raw your own conclusions as to how people change or why they change, but Xavian was a different kid than when he was born. In 2008, he was born with a fully functioning mind and body. By 2011, his abilities were compromised due to trauma inflicted upon his brain by a massive and aggressive tumor, which left the entire left side of his body weakened and his mind completely rewired. The way his mind processed thoughts and feelings, how he physically interacted with his environment, and what the world became to him was a very different thing from what it was when he started down the path of life. Whether he was designed to be born a certain way, then change into someone else is of no consequence. I love him for who he is and how he is. He's remarkable and I would never want to change his essence. He's capable of amazing things.

Through the power of imagination, I visited The Other Boy for quite some time. Minutes here felt like hours there. The more I thought about him, the bigger his world became. It fueled my imagination and would prove to serve a vital role in my healing.

The Other Boy looked a lot like Xavian. He had dark brown hair and an athletic body. He was a sweet kid, but also had an edginess about him. He hadn't faced any of the challenges Xavian had. For the most part, he was a typical kid, but certainly not without his struggles. Every kid struggles in some way, whether it's pronounced or not.

The Other Boy gifted his older brother a wrestling partner for those times when, well, you just had to lay it all on the line and see who the tougher guy was. Surely six-inch-thick cushions lined on the floor adjacently, forming a wrestling canvas, would protect a neck from a pile driver originating from the back-rest of the couch. Backyard brawls, bedroom bonanzas, and couch cushion competitions would most certainly end with a bruise, scrape, and plenty of tears. No call-out to mom was necessary. Tattling wasn't allowed. Things would be handled like men, right then and there. Natural consequences were always more fun. Although his older brother was a kinder, gentler fella, he retained his title as Champion of the Brothers more times than not. Older siblings have a way of being one step ahead in that regard.

The news of a baby sister was a bit concerning for The Other Boy, as he had wondered why his mother's belly looked so—well, big, and for quite some time, and why his father had spent more time with him than usual. He tried to make sense of it; I mean, how could a human live inside another human, and who in their right mind would put a small person inside another, larger person? He didn't know a belly could stretch that way. It looked so painful and seemed so...*cruel*. I'm sure it seemed alien, to him. Oh well, it didn't really matter. There were more important things to think about like candy bars, wrestling matches with big brother, and playing outside, plus he loved spending more time with dad. I don't think The Other Boy cared too much for his little sister when she arrived. She was always putting slimy, wet stuff from her mouth on him when he got close to her. Was it some sort of serum that got applied before the predator devoured its prey? That didn't seem right at all, but he was gentle with her nonetheless. He had no problem withdrawing from such a scarily dangerous situation. A war with slobber never ended well for him. His best bet was always to steer clear of her. It was most logical.

The Other Boy loved playing sports. He was so competitive. Despite dealing with the nipping anxiety that came about from team sports, he didn't mind taking the spotlight when the bright lights came on. The Other Boy was built for it, both physically and mentally. He loved competition and thrived off his opponent's energy. He gained momentum, not anxiety, from being an integral piece of a larger team. Sporting a tight fauxhawk with his dark brown hair, he gave off a strong vibe as a cool and tough character who wouldn't hesitate to bowl over an opponent at home plate if that's what it took to score. The only thing missing was a nice set of tattoos.

School was not too bad for The Other Boy. He fell in line with all the other kids, getting lost in the crowd like a chameleon in everything around him. He easily blended in. Sure, he had fears, anxiety, and general concerns, but he was able to cope with such things. On the playground, he led games of chase and hide-and-seek, and was usually the first one to notice the little girls who took interest in him. He didn't concern himself with the why, what, or how of things. He preferred to just go for it—and he did. As far as schoolwork was concerned, it was all pretty straightforward. They just told him what to do and he did it. He might not have been the smartest chap in town, but he was quite resourceful. He'd figure out a way to get the work done, then he'd think about sports, girls, and more important things. For him, school was a place to socialize. It was an institution where he just wanted to have fun, otherwise it was him against time, and he knew he'd never win that battle.

Video games provided a nice world for The Other Boy to get lost in. Whether playing a sports game where he could pretend to be the most popular professional player or embarking on an adventure to save the princess, he was up for the challenge. Of course, video games brought frustration in their own special way, so going outside for a bicycle ride was sometimes the best segue out of it.

The Other Boy had an appetite that rivaled a giant blue whale or a tiny pygmy shrew, which eats three times its own weight on a daily basis. When eating out, mom and dad knew better than to hand The Other Boy a kid's menu. The adult menu is where all the good stuff lived. Plus, the portions were larger. The type of food was of no concern to him. Whether the food was Italian, Latin, American, or anything in between didn't matter. "How does it taste?" was the question. Calories had been burned and a growling stomach demanded to be fed.

All the noises of the restaurant provided The Other Boy with sensory excitement. The various conversations amongst people around the restaurant provided him with entertainment. The louder it got, the more engaged he became. Eating out every Thursday night at the local pizza joint was an event he looked forward to each week. It was the loudest, most exciting, turbulent place he could imagine, not to mention it had the best food. All the pizza you can eat, an arcade, and a claw machine. What more could a kid ask for? There was so much more to explore with regard to The Other Boy, in his childhood, throughout his life, and into death, but time was working against me.

The Other Boy exists in my mind, in my heart, and perhaps in another dimension altogether. Regardless of when, where, how, and whether or not he exists at all, he feels real to me. I've imagined him as vividly as is humanly possible. I feel him through Xavian and I feel him in Xavian, and in myself. My time spent with The Other Boy heightened my excitement and increased my inspiration in Xavian. I truly believe I was given the gift of imagination, not to dream up impossible realities, but to unlock the gates which stand between what is right in front of me and a fascinating world where anything is possible. Being able to apply that gift to Xavian and his future is immeasurable.

The Other Boy and I had intriguing conversations about anything and everything. We talked about our favorite sports players and why we were so intrigued by them. We discussed why we liked certain video games, in comparison to other video games, and exactly what in the game fascinated us so profoundly. We debated whether pizza or Mexican cuisine was the better food. We conversed about Xavian. I explained all the amazing things Xavian had faced and conquered during his life, and how he was the bravest boy I'd ever met. The Other Boy wanted to meet Xavian, so I promised, if it was ever a possibility, I would most definitely make it happen. We spent many hours walking around the neighborhood, building forts down at the park, and exploring imagination more deeply. I even got to see one of his baseball games. I grew to truly understand him at a level I didn't think was possible. Understanding who The Other Boy was became the key to finding inspiration in Xavian. The moment I explored these emotions was the moment endless possibilities flowed freely right out of the heart of the internal war I'd been fighting.

This is not a story about what might have been. It's a story of the beauty in *what is*, and it's the reason I titled this book "The Other Boy." This book tells of an amazing, painful journey and the unlikely healing within that journey. From the moment I began journaling ideas for this book, until it was ready for publishing, the concept and healing power of The Other Boy is what touched me most deeply. It's symbolically the most important part of this journey for me, and perhaps other moms and dads on similar journeys will have the same opportunity. It's seeing your child and yourself from multiple perspectives, even if you have to travel far into your imagination to find the right viewpoint. Who knows, such a thing could be the most important part of your journey if you are able to see it, face it, grab a hold of it, and understand it.

There was no way to prepare for the adventure we were

thrust into way back in 2009, and I wasn't ready for my imagination to connect two worlds in the way it did ten years later so that I could begin healing, but I was never supposed to be ready. For certain things in life, preparation is simply impractical. It's never too late to start killing off the demons in our lives which seek to reduce, restrain, and shackle us to the weight of our own limitations.

MOVING ON

M y time spent with The Other Boy metamorphosed into an acceptance of reality. I needed to meet him and spend time with him. I longed to discuss life with him and deeply explore my emotions at the same time. Thoughts of what might have been were slowly transforming into a prison, my prison, and the longer I waited to escape, the less chance it seemed I would ever escape. I'm ever thankful for possessing the imagination necessary to step foot into a world in which I didn't belong. I'm also forever grateful for finding enough courage to explore the boundless depths of emotion which just as easily could have broken me for good. I was a train wreck, wrapped in a plane crash, shackled to a metal stake in the middle of the yard, and I desperately needed a way out of it.

Until we accept what kids like Xavian go through on a daily

basis, there will always be a need to think about kids like The Other Boy, so that our hope for them can be manifested. If we don't try to understand their situations by means of thought-provoking comparison and vision, then we will never be able to understand the gravity of what they're going through, and subsequently what their families are going through. The Other Boy became immensely important to me the moment I was able to figure out why I was sinking so deeply into his world, and believe me when I vehemently say—it was *his* world, of which I was merely a spectator. Those excursions became a vessel of hope in my life, when I otherwise would have accepted trivial limitations for Xavian's life and my own, allowing myself to become lazy, complacent, and accepting of defeat. **Instead, an entirely new world was opened up to me, and to Xavian through me.** My amazement in Xavian became a gift to him and it changed the game for me. It motivated me to spend more time with him and challenge him in ways I never would have before.

As awesome as The Other Boy was, he was never going to inspire people the way Xavian could. I visited The Other Boy for over a year, but I didn't understand the impetus for those visits at that time. I now know that it was an integral part of healing. It also served as a not-so-different view into myself as a child, which was helpful in many ways. The Other Boy served as a boost to my gratitude and humility. He helped soften my calloused heart, especially with regard to my unique, daily struggle as a father of a child with extremely challenging, atypical behavior.

Coming back was *tremendously* painful, but I was willing to deal with that pain the whole way back. As it is with most things in life though, there was a purpose behind the discomfort, and that purpose had been fulfilled. As much as I enjoyed visiting, learning, and feeling The Other Boy, I had to let him go. Once I realized I couldn't go back there, I was again forced to deal with the rejection and abandonment issues which have prodded me my entire life. That agony would be short lived though, because I knew it was time to take the next step in my journey as a father. As blessed as I was to get a glimpse of what Xavian could have been, the next step was to be truly grateful for who he really was, and push society's boundaries of what he could be. As such, that became my focus.

The last time I visited with The Other Boy, he told me I had already found what I was looking for and that I didn't need to keep coming to see him. As much as we had enjoyed our time together, and as painful as it was to admit it, our paths were diverging and it was time to move on. His world began fading out of existence. Astoundingly, this gift of imagination, which I had been told for years was an imaginary, useless ability, had just been used in a most prodigious and pragmatic way. I found great peace in that.

In the context of the abilities of one's children, that concept works both ways. If someone has children who are, for the most part, typical, they can try to imagine what it would be like to parent a child with special needs, or they can read stories like this one, or they can pay attention to what other families face on a daily basis. Likewise, if someone has a child who has special needs, they can imagine another version of that child and their role as a parent in that child's life from many different angles, then come back from that, just as I did. It might just help them to bring reality into focus and take a detour from the bumpy road they're on to a parallel path of healing.

Regardless of how parents see their children, or from which side of the fence they are peering over, seeking other perspectives is an enlightening way to open the mind's eye, to gain much more than a single, narrow view, and to become a better, more purposeful parent. Xavian is a special boy, and caring for him and being called upon for such a significant responsibility in the face of chaos has been an incredible honor for me.

As quickly as our lives had changed back in 2009, I had to depart from The Other Boy in 2019. Hardship had prepared me for an amazing journey, one which took me to a place far beyond the natural world we see in front of us. Coming back from that place brought me to an extraordinary destination—one of healing.

DAD

I n healthcare matters where a child is the patient, I believe medical professionals often focus the majority of their attention toward the mother instead of the father, even in situations where the father is present, attentive, and fully capable of processing every bit of information being exchanged. I also believe conditioning, not personal motive, is the reason for this. I'm not talking about physical conditioning, rather I'm talking about conditioning that stems from the fact that mothers are generally more nurturing, more attuned to the needs of their children, and fathers are often absent due to work demands, irresponsibility, or death. The natural consequence of this is that medical professionals can be subconsciously trained to focus on the mother only. This doesn't mean every single medical professional who interacts with parents of a patient will aim their focus in this manner, but in my experience, it is very common.

In my journey as a father through our many medical hurdles, I consistently felt completely *invisible* to medical professionals. This happened to me on numerous occasions, namely when Cassie and I were both present. To make matters worse, when they did acknowledge me, they often referred to me as "dad," which for some reason really annoyed me. Coupled with the fact that I can't always express myself as effectively as I would like, it was extremely frustrating. It's an organic, but unfortunate side effect for fathers like me, who not only willingly share leadership responsibilities with their wife, but are also highly attuned to the underlying mood, energy, and needs of our children.

This phenomenon isn't restricted to the confines of clinics, medical centers, hospitals, and the like. I experienced this feeling of invisibility in normal, everyday life among friends, family, and acquaintances too. It didn't happen a lot, only a handful of times, but it happened more than it should have and I could see it coming every single time. As I mentioned earlier in this book, during our stay at the hospital, or any of the stressful times in between, someone we knew would approach us and ask Cassie how she was holding up. Sometimes they wouldn't address me at all. I appreciated their concern for Cassie, as it always seemed genuine and heartfelt, but we were in the battle together. After waiting a few moments and realizing the other person may not even know I was standing there, a subtle smile would lock onto my face and my mind would wander into far-off places until the conversation ended. I would never bring up my observation or my hurt feelings to Cassie. It didn't seem necessary and there was nothing anyone could have done about it. I've always erred on the side of trying not to add more stress to someone who was already stressed, so I locked it in the safe and saved it for my writing.

My saving grace has been that, to the most important people in my life, Cassie and my children, I am both visible and vital. Cassie is a kind, sweet person who is as willing to share the leadership of our family with me as I am with her. She has also expressed her care for me over the years by placing herself in my shoes and showing empathy and courage that way. Difficult things in life require very specific types of courage. Writing a book requires the kind where an author spills their heart out to the rest of the world. Taking the first step into something difficult, which carries a low chance of success and a high chance of an all-out meltdown for a child who has special needs, takes massive amounts of courage. Cassie does things for Xavian that I struggle to find enough courage to initiate. Even though I'm more than happy to follow her lead on such matters, rarely am I the one taking the first step. I don't have her motherly intuition and I don't have her courage. The good news is, a person can be a leader and still be a follower. In fact, good followers make good leaders. More notably, good leaders know *when* to follow and *when* to lead, as well as *how* to follow and *how* to lead.

When it comes to my family, I will go anywhere and I will fight anyone for them. I am their warrior. If harm threatens them, then that harm will be cast out of our lives. That's how much I love my family. They are the precious, fragile cargo which I have been entrusted to protect. This journey and my time spent with Xavian has given me priceless insights and perspectives I otherwise may not have ever received, and I'm more thankful for that than I could ever express with words, written or spoken.

What jumps out at me the most as a father is how important tuning into our kids is. If we put down the smartphone, prioritize our hobbies (meaning we give our hobbies a lower priority than our children), and pay attention to them, we can know them and guide them. As a sensitive, intuitive father who has the ability to show love and leadership without asserting control over my kids and my family, I found that the more I showed Xavian patience, kindness, strength, optimism, but most of all love and gratitude, the better chance he had to turn toxic, destructive behavior into gentle compassion.

Throughout this journey, I've constantly explored ways to help Xavian overcome his seemingly insurmountable issues. It's extremely frustrating to have ideas that are squashed by financial or other roadblocks, or to have ideas that simply aren't feasible. Then there's the common problem I have as an outside the box thinker of coming up with ideas which are simply ahead of their time, and thus not possible yet. Regardless of the obstacles, I never stopped thinking of ways to overcome the challenges encountered along the way. Think of it as incessant troubleshooting.

Because of my high sensitivity, I'm easily overwhelmed by loud noises, strong smells, and things that don't feel good to the touch, like spit or things that feel mushy. Xavian's oft-continuous crying trampled my brain like a herd of wildebeests. Time spent around too many people quickly made me feel weak, light-headed, and sick to my stomach. When Xavian attempted self-harm, and I jumped in to protect him, he turned that aggression toward me, usually with clawing and spitting. Theoretically, I should have crumbled into microparticles somewhere along the way, but I didn't. I haven't.

Sure, I've had plenty of moments where I felt like an utter failure as a parent, but I made a decision to not give up on my son and I have no plans to come off of that decision. It's more than alright to struggle through something. I feel like sometimes people think that, if they aren't knocking whatever they're doing out of the park, then they aren't doing it right, but I don't subscribe to that mindset. A person's heart being in the right place through a difficult life event, or a journey like the one we've been on, is much more important than how well they feel they're doing at that thing. In life matters, the heart defines you, not some outward measure.

Regardless, it's not about success or failure, it's about dedication, love, courage, selflessness, and perseverance. With each step a father, mother, or caretaker takes in their journey, the past doesn't matter. Physics dictates that the past cannot be changed. What matters most is the next step. I want men to take that step as virtuous fathers through the lens of righteousness. I want them to crave their place, alongside their significant other, as a humble servant in their household. If I can brave a journey like the one I've been on, I know other fathers can too, and I believe they can do it better than I have.

In my thoughts, dreams, and imagination, it's as if I lived an entire life with The Other Boy. I knew him better than anyone can imagine. I saw how he thrived and how he struggled. I experienced his ups and downs. I saw who I would need to be for him. Better yet, I saw the version of me I could have ended up, that lazy one who watched from a distance while his son played by himself. I saw that withdrawn father who didn't see a need to provide deep emotional support and comfort to his son on a daily basis, who gave his son no leadership, no insights, and no direction in life. I saw that father who struggled immensely to simply connect with his son, and just assumed his son was alright when, on the inside, he was all wrong. I saw that father who subscribed to anything and everything society told him to in a narrow-minded state of mediocrity.

I have a son and a daughter who are considered typical, and one of them was born before the term "special needs" became such a permanent, blaring fixture in my life. I most assuredly was headed down one or more of those disappointing paternal paths I just mentioned. I understand how difficult the struggle can be, but I now know that the struggle of fatherhood doesn't have to dictate the execution of fatherhood. Understanding how things could have been is a powerful tool in changing the way things are.

NOT THE LAST

We weren't the first family to take a long, exhausting journey through childhood cancer and special needs, and we won't be the last. Unfortunately, these battles will continue as long as there are humans on Earth. If you are reading this book and are currently going through a similar journey, or just found out you will be soon, or you know someone who could use some encouragement, then you've come to the right place. I can't tell you how to make your experience pain-free, but I can share insights I've obtained during our journey.

My first piece of advice is to trust the system. Even though my trust in the system is a bit fractured, that doesn't mean yours has to be. My trust was already battle-hardened anyway. You really have no choice but to trust the system because, generally, you don't have another option. It's not as simple as Coke versus Pepsi. Any option you receive will come equipped with a recommendation. Unless you have some insight that refutes that recommendation, you'll probably be following it. So, trust the system, but hold them accountable. Pay close attention and research anything you don't understand or that doesn't sound right. Connect with other parents who are dealing with the same (or at least similar) things you are dealing with. There's an enormous amount of knowledge out there for you. There's also a great deal of support available to you if you are willing to express your need for it. Understand your options, when there *are* options, and make sure you understand any legal aspects that may affect you.

Second, you have to find what works for you. Some families live hours away from the hospital where their child will be receiving chemotherapy treatments, having scans or tests, visiting clinics, or all of the above. This can be problematic, but you have to weigh your options and visit every angle of the situation. Find people you can lean on and allow them to help you. Find your rhythm. For us, that meant alternating nights at the hospital and accepting the help of a few friends and family members. Alternating nights may not be the best approach for you, but there *is* something that will work best for you. I suggest you find it. Don't be afraid to try different things. If you're married, discuss it with your spouse. Talk with each other about the things that bring stress. Pay attention to your spouse and try to get a feel for what works for them and what doesn't. If you don't know, ask them. Don't be afraid to try something new for them, even if it makes you uncomfortable. For some of you, selflessness will be your best friend.

I also highly recommend journaling your experience. When we started on this journey, I was very excited about capturing my thoughts during a time of distress. Up until the time Xavian was diagnosed with a brain tumor, I'd always loved writing, but never had the focus or a reason to write. When he got sick, I had multiple reasons to write. First and foremost, writing was therapeutic for me. Each time I logged an update to our journal, I felt a sense of freedom and relief. Second, we had friends and family dispersed in various areas, and since I hated talking on the telephone, journaling to a place where our friends and family could easily get updates on Xavian quickly became a very good reason to write.

Sadly, as quickly as my fire for journaling was ignited, it was even more quickly extinguished. My stress was increasing, and at the time, I was struggling. Not all was lost though. Inspired by my journaling, Cassie picked up where I left off without skipping a beat, and she was really good at it. She's not a writer, nor does she claim to be, but Cassie is the most genuine person I've ever met, and that virtue shone brightly through her writing. She logged journal entries for over three years.

Most of our journals were captured on Caring Bridge, which is a personal health journaling site with a single vision—create a world where no one goes through a health journey alone, accompanied by a simple, but profound mission—build bridges of care and communication, providing love and support on a health journey. This book would not have been written without those journals. The paralyzing effect of the stress we faced on our journey, coupled with the fact that my memory is sketchy at best, made our journals critical for the telling of this story. The great thing about journaling is it's quick and straightforward, and anyone can do it.

Next, you'll want to embrace the perspectives which become available to you throughout your journey. They are priceless. Being able to experience things from different angles, especially when those experiences are painful, can fill you with empathy. You have to allow yourself to be broken down and put back together. Don't be afraid of being broken down and your heart softened. Empathy struggles to survive in a hardened heart. If your journey is like ours, then there will be ample opportunity for your heart to be hardened, but there will be equal, if not more, opportunity for your heart to be softened. That's when new perspectives become visible and empathy becomes an option.

Finally, expect there to be pain. It's going to hurt and it's going to be scary, and if you can grab that five-hundred-pound mass of pain by the horns, you will rule the world. Many of us can't see the future, so we assume the worst. While you're in pain, try to think about why you're in pain and how you can use that pain to better understand the purpose behind it. Purpose can always be found in pain. In fact, pain can't exist without purpose. Don't expect to be awestruck at every corner, but do what you must in order to take care of your family while pain is doing everything it can to stop you. Taking care of your family while staring pain right in the eye will unlock the most precious purpose imaginable—giving up will not.

Mistakes will be made. You will struggle. Endless rivers of tears will flow from you. Fundamental things like self-care will prove difficult. Some days, simply talking will seem pointless. Don't expect to be at your best. Expect to feel numb, but don't give up. As long as you are there, caring for your family, fighting for them, and seeking purpose in it, amazing things will happen. Remember, your family is a gift regardless of the circumstances surrounding your daily walk. Days, weeks, even years will be exhausting in the midst of emotional angst and physical suffering. You can find gratitude in that, and the burden will only walk through the door when you allow it to by giving your heart to things which pull you away from that gratitude.

Whether it's you or someone you know who is going

through a similar journey as ours, remember there is a reason for the hardship. Don't let the overwhelming pain, which sticks with you every step of the way, negate the fact that you have been commissioned to do something larger than life. Your pain is real, there's no denying it. That pain also seems big, but the purpose behind it is bigger. You're going to lose parts of yourself during your journey. And you might lose all of yourself, but not all is lost. There will be opportunities for you to find yourself again. Don't be afraid to look deeply into the heart of what you do best for the answers you need. Instead of struggling with things that cripple you, focus on those things with which you shine most brightly, and dive into it. The parts of you that have been misplaced are waiting to be rescued— by you. You owe it to yourself and your family to put yourself back together and be ever more strengthened in that.

WONDER WOMAN

Have you ever met someone who, no matter the circumstances, just seems like a superhero? In sports, they call this the Most Valuable Player, the MVP. In just about every sport, each year one player earns the title of MVP due to their consistent excellence throughout the long, demanding season. Notably, only one player can be designated as the MVP. This doesn't mean there weren't a handful of others who achieved excellence as well, it just means one player achieved a level of excellence which stood out the most.

I thought about this chapter for many months. I racked my brain on how I could thank each individual who touched our family in a heartfelt way. I wrote this chapter, then I deleted it, then I wrote it again and deleted that too. I even started a chapter where I tried to thank every single person I could think of, but with my erratic memory that most assuredly would not have turned out the way I wanted.

If you are someone who has made a significant effort during our strenuous adventure, know that we know you made such an impact, forever blessing us, and we are eternally grateful to you for that. There are simply too many kind souls to mention, and my biggest fear was about the short list, the short list of kind souls who I would have inadvertently omitted in trying to name them all. I couldn't live with myself after committing such an unforgivable offense.

So, just as they do in sports, I decided the most considerate path would be to pick the person who, without question, was our MVP during our journey through childhood cancer and special needs. Her name is Sasha and she is an Acute Care Pediatric Nurse Practitioner at Children's Hospital of Alabama.

Sasha received her initial undergraduate degree in Biology and eventually became involved with Smile-A-Mile in 2001, when she decided her heart was drawn to pediatric oncology. It was at that point that she began to pursue a second degree in nursing. By 2005, Sasha had completed her registered nursing (RN) degree from UAB. Shortly thereafter, she joined the PICU team at Children's Hospital of Alabama. She chose PICU in order to obtain a broad spectrum of knowledge. She cared for patients in PICU for the next six years.

After Xavian's tumor resection surgery in 2009, he was admitted to the PICU at Children's Hospital. That's where we first met Sasha. I don't remember as much about that time as I'd like because I was basically in shock, but I do remember a few of the nurses, including Sasha, who was thirty-six weeks pregnant and whose personality jumped right off the screen. During the writing of this book, I crafted a few questions in an email message for her so that I could add a bit more substance to this chapter in an attempt to supplement my poor memory. The last of those questions was, "What do you remember about Xavian when he first came into PICU?" I *never* sent the question to her, however. I just wasn't sure if that was the direction I wanted to go with this chapter, so I deleted it. As fate would have it, at the end of her reply to my email message containing the other questions, Sasha provided an answer to the question I never sent. It read like this:

"I will never forget when working in PICU the day Xavian was admitted. He was 11 weeks old and I was 36 weeks pregnant with my first child, who was a boy. I will never forget having to walk to our break room to take a breather. I prided myself on being able to separate my emotions from my work, but in Xavian's case it was just not possible. Cassie's blank "deer in headlights" stare is something that is ingrained in my memory forever. Love you guys so much and I have been honored to play a small role in your journey."

It seems sometimes small roles make titanic-sized impacts. I believe in spiritual connections and I believe, in that moment, when Sasha met Xavian for the first time, a spiritual connection was formed between herself and our family.

In May of 2010, Sasha received her Master's in Nursing degree from UAB. Having always known she would go into pediatric oncology, she moved from PICU to the Hematology/Oncology clinic (Clinic 8) once a position became available. There, she worked closely with the neuro-oncologists. Back in 2009, when Xavian was in PICU for only a few days, we didn't get to spend much time with Sasha, but once she moved to Clinic 8, we saw her often. Seeing Sasha on a regular basis, in my mind at least, was the equivalent to finding a hidden treasure in a secret world. We saw the passion and focus she devoted to other patients and we felt that passion deeply when she gifted the same to Xavian and our family.

I remember initiating the following conversation with Xavian recently.

"Hey Xavian, do you remember Sasha?" I started.

"Yes, from Children's Hospital," he replied.

"That's right. What do you think about her?"

"Great."

You'd have to know Xavian to understand that "great" is the highest compliment a person could ever receive from him.

Sasha embodies this extremely unique combination of intelligence, competence, strength, excitement, leadership, relatability, passion, encouragement, practicality, love, and hope. I don't believe I've ever met anyone with such strong social, interpersonal, and people skills in my entire life. She seemed to fully grasp the concept of boundaries, which is often a very delicate and tricky concept to navigate. For us, she was the epoxy that held everything together when it felt like the crumbling of our world around us could not be stopped. Every single time we visited Clinic 8, or got to spend time with Sasha at the Crawfish Boil in her neighborhood, or randomly ran into her around town, whatever darkness or negative energy was present was immediately whisked away and replaced with the light and positive energy she exuded. She warmed the room with the sunlight of her soul.

Sasha made you feel like you were the only person in the room, and I'm certain Xavian felt that deeply. She made our family feel special, which is how every family fighting cancer deserves to feel. I'm certain she made every family feel that way. What I loved the most about Sasha's interaction with Xavian is that when she started a conversation with him, she committed to it. She didn't ask him one question, ignore his answer, then focus on Cassie or myself while almost pretending he wasn't in the room, as so many others in the field of patient care had done in the past. She engaged with him, committing to the conversation and following through with the interaction. It was not only a sign that she cared for her patients, but a reflection of her incredibly strong interpersonal skills. There were quite a few historic conversations between Sasha and Xavian, but my favorite conversation went like this:

"Hey Xavian!" Sasha exclaimed as she entered our room during a scheduled checkup in Clinic 8.

"Hey, you look like Wonder Woman," Xavian responded with a big smile.

We were all left speechless for a moment as Sasha stood still with her eyes big and her mouth opened wide in amazement. I could see her mind racing, searching for a response, but for a moment not finding one.

"Wait, which one? The old one or the new one?" Sasha asked.

"The new one," Xavian responded, as if there was any doubt.

"You're my new favorite person Xavian."

During our next visit to Clinic 8, as Sasha greeted us in our room, Xavian surprised us all again as he looked at Sasha and interrupted, "Hey. I care for you deeply." There was a momentary pause covered in awe. The soul of every adult in that room turned to jelly and our hearts melted. I'm certain Sasha shed a few tears over it later.

From that point forward, Sasha proudly owned the title of "Wonder Woman," a label befitting such a warrior.

I'll never forget the day when Xavian was a toddler, when he gave everyone in the Clinic 8 waiting room the concert of a lifetime. Actually, it was just one short song. His song of choice was "I Love Colors." Xavian sang it loudly and in tune, and his version went something like this:

"Boogers are red

Roses are blue

I love colors yes I do

I love colors yes I do

Purple and green and yellow too

Colors, colors, I love all the colors

Go go go go rainbows, in my head

Green and blue"

What followed was applause by everyone in the waiting room with one older lady turning to her friend and asking, "Did he say boogers are red?" We were dying with laughter. It was one of those moments I'll never forget, mostly because it was a happy moment, and a moment where we felt free and loose. I'll also never forget the look on Sasha's face when she walked out into the waiting room and just froze about a third of the way through the song. The excitement she exuded epitomized her genuineness and uplifting spirit we grew to admire and anticipate so deeply.

In 2019, we made our last scheduled trip to Clinic 8. After ten years of going there, we were done. It was bitter-sweet, but mostly sweet. While the staff were all wonderful and supportive, the reality was we were visiting a hospital. Who genuinely wants to visit a hospital? The answer is no one. No one wants to visit a hospital. Xavian had just finished his last scheduled MRI a few days earlier, and if those scans showed no evidence of disease, he would be graduating from Clinic 8. That day was sweet for two reasons.

Firstly, Xavian wouldn't require any more expensive, anxiety-inducing, annoying MRIs or Clinic 8 visits. Secondly, on the day of that last visit, as it had been on a few occasions previously, there was just Sasha and us in the room. If a doctor came in, I don't remember it. Ever since Xavian's primary neuro-oncologist moved away a few years earlier, I don't remember much of any other doctor in Clinic 8. I just remember Sasha. It was special because she was special to us. It was bitter in that we wouldn't be seeing her on a regular basis any more.

No one knows this, but I shed tears that day, right there in our room. They couldn't see because, while the attention was on

Xavian, I wiped the tears away. I was just overcome with so much gratitude that day. I was so thankful for the wonderful people we spent time with throughout our journey, especially Sasha. I found it fitting that we ended that phase of our journey in such a beautifully intimate manner. It was like a nice sunset—poetic.

Have you ever heard the expression, "I'm a better person because I know you"? I can say, today, without a doubt I'm a better person because I know Sasha and I'm certain Cassie shares that sentiment. There are people in this world who make me never want to speak to another person. Sasha has the *opposite* effect. She makes me want to pay forward the joy which she has always freely and organically emitted. My only regret is that we didn't get to spend more time with her. With all due respect to the wonderful nurses and nurse practitioners who visited our room on a daily basis way back in 2009 when Xavian was receiving chemotherapy, I can't help but to believe wholeheartedly that those long, exhausting, dark days on Four Tower would have been a bit better had we been visited by Sasha, who was at home starting her own beautiful family at the time. We need more people like her in this world and in our lives. The healthcare system in America needs more people like her.

Our professional relationship with Sasha ended in 2019, but as gifts go, all was not lost. By that time, our family had developed a friendship with her, which we were tremendously thankful for. Running into Sasha around town, attending events she helped organize, or just seeing her family pictures and videos on social media always brings a smile to our faces. Like the diamond which remains after the coal has been broken away, we are forever grateful.

GUILT

Guilt is that nagging little dink situated inches away from my ear, breathing disgusting, hot, moist insults and lies directly into my soul, as every bit of confidence I possess oozes out of me like ear wax. It is the bane of my existence.

Guilt is defined as "a feeling of having done wrong or failed in an obligation." What makes guilt so irrationally annoying is that it doesn't discriminate between people who are actually guilty and those who are not. For example, if someone commits a crime, they might carry guilt about the crime which they committed, regardless of whether or not they were caught. Conversely, if someone performs a good deed and it doesn't go the way they expected or isn't received in a way they had hoped, they might carry guilt about that outcome.

Regarding the latter, this guilt may serve a purpose initially, but can soon thereafter become a major annoyance to the person. That person may even begin to avoid situations which might make them feel guilty. They may also become remorseful or apologetic in situations where they should have laid down a hard boundary or denied any further advancements from someone or something. When guilt reaches this point, it's referred to as *neurotic guilt.* Neurotic guilt is guilt that has stopped serving as a useful moral compass and has started to become aggression turned against oneself. It's a type of guilt that is disproportionate to any wrongdoing, and often carries an obsessive responsibility for no rational reason. The most disheartening thing about it is it feels just like run of the mill, warranted guilt.

If I said I've never thought about losing one of my children to death, I'd be lying. In fact, if I said I hadn't played such an event and all that follows over and over in my head, thinking about what I would say, who would be there, how much my heart would ache, and the tears that would be shed, I'd be lying. Hence my vision I described in beginning chapter of this book, "The Gathering." I'm an overthinker, so I think about those types of things, so much so that the tears don't have to wait for such an occasion. The tears can come now—and they do, on demand, whenever I wish. I think about what life would be like without one of my children and how, at times, it seems like it would be a more comfortable and much simpler life. I'm sure it would be.

Guilt-inducing thoughts like that weigh heavier on my heart and soul than any six-thousand-pound elephant ever could. Logic, however, offers up a different reality and constantly reminds me that life without one of my children would consist of a gaping hole in my heart, in Cassie's heart, and in the hearts of our entire family. Regret and grief would feed my heart's guilt more quickly and tenaciously than I could contain. That's the shiftiness of guilt though. It sometimes tries to play the role of love and stake a claim to the purity of love, but it's nothing like love.

Conversely, I wonder sometimes if guilt actually requires love in order to exist. Being a parent in general is taxing and organically guilt-inducing. Just the thought of bringing a child into a world where they are immediately thrust into a life full of disadvantages, with guilt surrounding discipline, guilt associated with not spending enough time with them because the energy requirements are so acute and demanding, and guilt that I'm simply too inadequate to be a father, weighs quite heavy. There's nothing more humbling than the latter. I like to believe it's because I love them so much, not because I've made so many mistakes, but guilt won't have it. It harasses me with a constant nipping.

Not long after Xavian was diagnosed with a brain tumor, I

remember several fathers, who also had children with cancer diagnoses, sharing with me how guilty they felt. I remember thinking, "YES! That's exactly how I feel." There was this terrible, remorseful, and physically harmful feeling boiling inside me, constantly tugging at me, sending sharp, irritating pulses of electricity up my neck. Until those fathers put it into words, I couldn't identify it. It was guilt, and it was the unwarranted variety. I hadn't done anything wrong.

I went to most of the obstetrician (OB) visits with Cassie when she was pregnant with each of our kids. I was there for the birth of all of our children, including Xavian's. It was never a question of whether I'd be there, only a question of how many awkward things I would say to give the room its most uncomfortable mood possible. I'm sure I did not disappoint. I was there, much to the dismay of my intuition, the day we knew something was wrong with Xavian and spent over eight hours in the emergency room. But it didn't matter. Neurotic guilt was landing haymakers on me, as if it were training for a heavyweight fight and I was merely its sparring partner, or better yet, its punching bag. This type of guilt can be suppressed with an assist from time, but it never truly goes away. I have experienced neurotic guilt throughout my life, but never remotely as overwhelmingly as I have with regard to Xavian and all that he's been through.

My neurotic guilt isn't limited to Xavian though. I may be the only father on our journey, but I'm joined by my wife and three kids. I have experienced first-hand how Cassie is affected on a daily basis, first by childhood cancer and now, perhaps more significantly, by special needs. I do everything within my being to lighten her personal load in this battle, often nearing the boundaries of my own sanity. When Cassie is out somewhere getting a break from the chaos at home, I don't text or call her to tell her how badly things are going with Xavian. I don't want to add stress to those precious moments where she is trying to relax and re-energize. She deserves peace of mind for as long as it's available to her and it's up to me to ensure she experiences it. It's still not enough. She staggers on. We stagger on. And the guilt prods me every step of the way. The "If I had only" and "I should have" thoughts pierce loudly with an irrational voice. They don't hold back.

When I was a kid, the word "retarded" was tossed around like salad. Thinking about that now, where the definition of the word retarded—less advanced in mental, physical, or social development than is usual for one's age—applies perfectly to my own son, makes me feel as sick as if I had eaten an expired salad. The guilt for my past self's behavior is sharp, and I'm sometimes irrationally resentful of anyone else who negligently used the word back then. "Special needs" wasn't a thing when I was a kid. *Retarded was.*

If a person was slow, or had a learning disability, or anything else that made them seem less capable than others, they were labeled retarded. If a fully-capable person did something silly or stupid, or someone just didn't like them, they were deemed retarded. The word was diminishing to the person it was directed at, and to those who had real mental challenges, too. I am thankful for an age of political correctness where words like "mental disability" and "special needs" can't be haphazardly tossed around like "retarded" was back then. The words simply don't lend themselves to such futility. I'm also thankful for parents who teach their kids about inclusion and equality, and who will settle for nothing less than excellence when it comes to their children treating others with respect and kindness, especially kids who are differently-abled.

There's also the matter of shame and its relationship with guilt. Brené Brown stated it beautifully in her TED Talk titled "Listening to Shame."

"Shame is a focus on self, guilt is a focus on behavior," she says. "Shame is, 'I am bad.' Guilt is, 'I did something bad.' How many of you, if you did something that was hurtful to me, would be willing to say, 'I'm sorry. I made a mistake?' How many of you would be willing to say that? Guilt: I'm sorry. I made a mistake. Shame: I'm sorry. I am a mistake."

Brown goes on to say, "Shame is highly, highly correlated

with addiction, depression, violence, aggression, bullying, suicide, and eating disorders. Here's what you even need to know more: Guilt is inversely correlated with those things. The ability to hold something we've done, or failed to do, up against who we want to be is incredibly adaptive. It's uncomfortable, but it's adaptive."

I grew up in South Jackson, Mississippi in the suburbs. Back in those days, most kids were allowed to roam the streets, all day long if they so desired, and I did. There was a church just a couple blocks over from our home. The church owned over thirty acres of land, which was squeezed in tightly between the church and Interstate 20. The land was partially wooded, with several large open fields and a softball field. The wooded area consisted mostly of pine trees, with a single trail winding through it from the south end, downhill, all the way to the north end near the interstate.

The fields consisted of long-bladed grass that stood several feet tall and danced vibrantly anytime the wind blew. This land, better known as The Ballpark, was my second home. It had everything I needed. Bicycle trails, plenty of branches and wood with which to build forts and tree houses, places to hide from strangers, and a small creek to play in. There was even an old youth building that had apparently been overtaken by devil worshipers. We did not attend this church.

I spent countless hours at The Ballpark contemplating the

universe and just being a kid. I was one of the only kids in the area who had enough imagination to entertain myself for an entire day at The Ballpark—and I certainly did. All the time. Rarely could another kid match my imagination, but there was a boy named Philip who might have been more creative than I was. He lived one street over from us and was what we refer to today as being intellectually disabled. In today's terms, we would say Philip had special needs.

Regardless of label, in some respects, he was brilliant. He had a flamboyant imagination, which usually manifested itself in some military role play. I lost track long ago of how many times I saw Philip leading an imaginary army down the street, around the corner, and straight onto the battlefield, marching and chanting every step of the way. He was a big kid; he towered over me. He was a little on the heavy side and always had a workmanlike aura about him. He seemed to always be on an important mission and usually provided me with highly classified, crucial nuggets of information that needed to be kept safe in case the North Vietnamese were to take him out before he could deliver it to the high command. Did I mention he had an impressive imagination?

Like me, Philip roamed the neighborhood as if he owned the place, going wherever he wanted, whenever he wanted, more so in the summertime than any other time of year. Our interactions were usually short and sweet, but I wasn't always kind to Philip. I wasn't a bully, but I also wasn't the supportive, nurturing kid who I expect others to be with Xavian. I was a hard-nosed kid who really just wanted to be left alone, and if Philip crossed me when I was struggling, then I would intentionally do things to irritate him and get him fired up, which I was skilled at.

The mental prodding I inflicted upon him was unfair, unwarranted, and quite frankly unsafe for me. Philip was the strongest kid around and could have easily hurt me without fully grasping what he was doing. Part of me wishes he had hurt me, but not too seriously, as a wake-up call. I could definitely feel his indignation toward me at times, but it never happened. Older, wiser kids in the neighborhood called me out regarding my treatment of Philip several times with pleas of wisdom, logic, and humanity. It may sound innocent enough, but I've carried a lot of guilt about my interactions with Philip over the years, the same kind of neurotic guilt which should have long since been dealt with, but refuses to leave nonetheless. Early on, I may have mistaken this feeling for shame, but it is undoubtedly guilt. I wasn't a terrible person, but what I did was a terrible thing. That is guilt.

Ironically, that guilt was dealt a huge blow while Xavian was receiving his chemotherapy treatments and I struggled in a dark, cold, lonely hospital room. Back in those days, I was on Facebook. It was a place where I could write notes and share them with anyone I was connected with, so friends, family, and strangers alike could know my problems. It was both frightening and therapeutic. One of the people who connected with me on Facebook was none other than Philip, the intellectually disabled kid from the old neighborhood, who I had not treated with the level of respect and worth he deserved those many years ago.

In 2009, we were both adults, and although it was quite difficult to get a feel for where he was in life and generally how he was doing, it was obvious he felt as connected to me as I did to him. Philip would occasionally reach out to me through text messages and inquire as to the health of my son. Occasionally, he would reflect on the old days. He also encouraged me. At first, it was perplexing.

"This guy should hate me. He shouldn't be expressing sympathy or concern for me or any of my offspring. He should be cursing me out, if anything," I pondered in confusion, as my neurotic guilt struggled to maintain the veil it had placed over my eyes many years prior.

Upon further review, as I was able to reach seemingly unreachable places in my soul and ultimately in my memory, a painful truth shone brightly. Guilt had blinded me to the fact that, as a teenager in high school, years after those days of roaming the neighborhood and being a maddening menace to Philip, I had turned things around with respect to how I treated him. In high school, I watched out for Philip. I protected him, hypocritically yet nobly willing to fight anyone who dared to treat him the way I once had. I got in the face of a few people who quickly sensed the guilt-induced fire burning inside of me. I caught my missteps early in life and atoned for my transgressions, honoring and respecting Philip during those high school years. His empathy toward me many years later affirmed what guilt had made me forget. It was guilt that had let me live with those lies for so many years.

Aside from imagining the potential death of my children, I have other suitcases full of guilt about things that haven't happened, and some that may never happen. The thought of Xavian having to live without Cassie or myself around to care for him is extremely guilt-inducing. Even though we've made plans for him to be cared for by caring people, there is still anxiety. Naturally, parents die before their kids, but I can't imagine that scenario for Xavian. The thought of us being gone, and things going off the rails for him, is deeply painful. I've heard horror stories of adults with special needs being mistreated in group homes and it shatters my heart into a thousand pieces. I also can't imagine burying Xavian. Therefore, I'm only left with one hope regarding death, that we all go together. As morbid as it sounds, it is a valid concern and an equally compassionate wish.

I don't know that I'll ever shake the thick, hard-shelled lay-ers of neurotic guilt I carry with me as the father of a child who I was commissioned to bring into the world, who was immediately dealt a dump truck load full of disadvantages and dependencies which most of us will never experience. I'm not sure I have to shake the guilt though. As long as I know, in my heart of hearts, guilt is a liar, then guilt will be the one living the lie, not me. The battle will wage on.

ALWAYS A GIFT

The question of "why" frequently pops into my head. I look for the "why" in things as opposed to the "what" or "how." I like to understand the reason for things, especially for things which invoke strong or impactful emotions. I believe, in a lot of situations, I may not want the answer to "why." It's not always an easy answer to swallow, but it's often necessary and can be constructive. The answer to, "Why did we go on this journey through childhood cancer and special needs?" is so incredibly complex and I'm not sure I'll ever be able to effectively unpack it. I'm not sure I could ever fully understand the gravity of it—it feels *that* heavy to me. I'm willing to bet no one wants their child to go through hell just so they're an inspiration to friends and complete strangers. I certainly did not.

However, as I've said before, pain and suffering have purpose. Deep, hidden meaning lies buried within, waiting to be unearthed, waiting to explode into enlightenment. This purpose always brings with it a gift. It's excruciating to watch our kids suffer, but if we can just slow down and go deeper into our souls, through whatever means necessary, then we can find that gift. For me, finding purpose in pain is the ultimate gift, and as I've gotten older, it's something I don't mind searching for. It can be scary, but what do we have to fear? Most great things in life are going to come by way of something uncomfortable. Look for the gift. It often lies snuggled down right in the core of the discomfort, pain, and suffering. One of the great ironies of life is finding the most beautiful things in the ugliest places, a pattern which never ceases to amaze me.

Have you ever thought about fear, like really thought about it? I have. I've come to the conclusion that fear is an illusion which serves as a tool. Fear is a bit of a truth stretcher, but not quite a lie. It's that tiresome filter that paints a much scarier, direr picture than what reality yields. It is clever at making us focus on a single moment, picking our lowest periods, and slowing time to an excruciating crawl. It puts up imaginary walls which cannot be scaled or knocked down, and somehow seem to stretch all the way around the world, blinding us from the great beyond. Fear would have us believe the apocalypse exists beyond those walls, when in reality there is beautiful, unfettered life on the other side.

Oddly enough, we can't seem to shake fear. In the movie *The Croods*, the dad, Grug says, "Never not be afraid." His entire existence has been built around the fear of change. In his world, if you remain afraid, you stay alive. You don't die like The Gorts, who were smashed by a mammoth; or The Horks, who were swallowed by a sand snake; or the Erfs, who were shish kabobbed by a mosquito; or The Throgs, who died by way of the common cold. By the end of the movie, Grug realizes, in order to experience new things, fear must be eliminated from the equation. It's the epitome of open-mindedness and perspective-seeking, and it encourages agility.

Because of our journey through childhood cancer and special needs, my life has demanded open-mindedness and agility for quite some time now. Settling into a single, narrow perspective at any point in our adventure didn't seem sensible to me. Don't get me wrong. I can be as afraid as the next guy, but I choose to fight it. Fighting fear doesn't mean you're not afraid of it, it just means you have made a choice to stand against it instead of allowing yourself to be steamrolled. Inevitably, fear sometimes gets the best of us, but the more we make conscious decisions to look it in the face, the more courageous we become. Courage is a virtue. It is moral strength in the face of danger.

GRACE

I would be extremely remiss to tell a story such as ours and not talk about grace. The word has a few different meanings, but the one I'm referring to revolves around freely giving (or receiving) favor to (or from) someone, whether it's merited or not. The distribution of grace to others is something society frowns upon. Society would rather have us demean people by placing a dunce cap on their head and have them sit on a stool in the corner of a room if they do any little thing we don't like. Cancel culture is a great example of this. Don't get me wrong, there are times when we must distance ourselves from others, but it can and should be done without forming a mob and slaughtering them like helpless lambs. It should be done with grace.

In 2017, my truck turned sixteen years old. Other than the dashboard, which was dry rotting from baking in the sun all those years, the truck was in great shape, both mechanically and aesthetically. It had never been scratched, side-swiped, or hit by another vehicle in any way. Even though it rarely received a bath, it looked good. Then one day, on a Thursday morning, a gentleman delivered a load of wood for my fence from a local lumber yard. As I stood twenty feet behind where I wanted the wood to be dropped, the driver backed slowly into my driveway, with reverse beepers blaring loudly like cicadas. As the truck neared a stop, the driver jumped out and quickly pulled a lever which caused the front of the trailer to slowly rise, allowing the wood to slide gracefully off the back of the trailer. Once the wood slid almost completely off the trailer, the driver jumped back in and nudged it forward a few times, allowing the wood to slide the rest of the way onto the ground.

I found this method intriguing and clever, and wanted to try it myself. Once the wood was on the ground, the driver jumped out of the truck and began walking back toward me. Fear struck me like lightning, chill bumps racing from my head all the way down to my toes.

I nearly fainted as I struggled to speak, but I was able to muster up, "Your truck is moving! Your truck is moving!" as I hopped up and down like a rabbit with my right index finger doing the walk of life.

The driver had forgotten to put the truck back in park

when he jumped out—a significant error indeed. He was an older man who looked like he was in his mid-60s, but reacted with cat-like reflexes not expected of a man his age. It was impressive, but it wasn't enough. As his truck quickly gained momentum, in a moment where time slowed to a crawl for me, I closed my eyes and titled my head toward the ground. I knew it was too late and I couldn't watch. My poor truck of only sixteen years of age, which was parked next to the street, would be bulldozed by a truck three times its size and there was absolutely nothing I could do about it.

As the massive lumber truck plowed into my half-ton pickup like an elephant trampling a rhino, my truck was tossed about, spun around, and pushed into the middle of the street. Surely this was the automotive version of bullying. I could only hope the damage was minimal. After being walloped repeatedly from a series of jolts and recoil, my truck was able to halt the stampeding mammoth, preventing it from charging across the street and into my neighbor's home. This was the silver lining a person needs in such a situation—a look on the bright side.

The driver, who had given all he had to stop the truck, was thrown violently to the ground. He appeared unharmed physically, but devastated emotionally. I immediately felt extraordinary panic and regret, radiating from somewhere deep within his soul. Aside from my truck being mauled, I felt for him. He was so upset he could barely speak. I'm certain that was the first time anything like that had ever happened to him. It was such a bizarre mistake and he genuinely seemed to know what he was doing. As the two trucks sat still in the middle of the road like a scene out of an action film, I looked around for a hidden camera crew, but found none. I tried to comfort him while he gathered himself, and then he started negotiating with me to not contact his company about what had just happened, as he feared he would be relieved of his duties.

I threw my hands up as if I were pushing a door open and said, "Listen, this is not a big deal. I'm not going to call your company. We'll figure it out ourselves."

He insisted I get a quote to fix my truck and allow him to pay for the damages, gave me his phone number, and he left. My truck had a large dent on the side of the bed, but was otherwise unscathed, and the larger truck didn't have a scratch on it. I never called my insurance company, but I did call him back a few days later and told him not to worry about anything, that he didn't owe me for the damage. I heard God say one thing, "Give him grace." So that's what I did. I was fully at peace with that, and the rest was easy.

God provides grace, sometimes proxying it through us to give to others. It's sort of His specialty. If gratitude is the effect, then grace is most certainly the cause. Bound to linear time, cause and effect always follow proper order. In this same breath, grace is given, first, then gratitude follows. That is the relationship I've experienced. Grace is infinite, therefore it is not limited to certain outcomes. Strangely enough, I never truly knew what grace was until Cassie explained it to me when I was thirty years old. Up until that point, I had lived a life where things like self-preservation and vengeance seemed more logical than grace, but we're never too old to learn elementary lessons. The fact that people needed grace so much had never truly sunk into my heart prior to that, but I was thankful to begin the trek into a deeper understanding of it.

February 4, 2018, is a day I will never forget. That's the day Xavian's Super-Nurse Alison, because she was always so much more than "just a nurse" to us, had a puppy party for her Boston terrier, Winnie. By this time, Alison was no longer Xavian's hematology and oncology nurse, but our neighbor and friend. One might wonder what a puppy party entails. It's simple. There's a puppy treat truck, which shows up at a dog park, and the dogs eat treats and mingle. What more could a pup ask for?

We were at Red Mountain Park, which hosts a network of impressive hiking trails, a variety of native plants and trees, and close to one hundred bird species. Red Mountain Park got its name from the red soil, which is tinted by the iron ore deposits that were once mined there as a major local industry in the 1800s. Red

Mountain Park also hosts a dog park, which sits on the southeast side. It's called Remy's Dog Park, and consists of large, small, and special needs dog areas. Visiting Remy's was always a blast. Well, not always. There was this one day, at Winnie the Dog's puppy party, where our trip took an unexpected turn.

After arriving that day, where the puppy treat truck was parked out front, my family separated for a bit. While Xavian and I took our goldendoodle, Finn, a few hundred yards down a trail in the woods to the dog park, Cassie, Larkin, and Dante remained near the puppy treat truck to mingle with friends. It just so happened that one of our neighbors was at Remy's that day, so she and I chatted for a few moments. As we stood still, talking on one side of the large dog park, Finn wandered around independently, sniffing anything that sparked his curiosity. Xavian also wandered around, most likely looking for shadows. As the conversation with my neighbor neared its end, I noticed a peculiar look of confusion in her eyes before she froze. Puzzled, I crinkled my brow, cocked my head slightly to the side, then slowly turned in the direction she was looking.

I was immediately overcome by panic. I briefly panned to the left of where my neighbor was focused and saw a group of five strangers with the same look. Finally seeing what they were looking at, electricity shot through my being. With butterflies in my stomach, I didn't know what to do, so I did what any grown man would do. I began flapping my arms like a sea lion, as if to say, "PLEASE NO!" while I hesitantly moved in the direction of the commotion. I'm not sure if my neighbor heard me, but what I said to her was, "I've got to go. I'll see you later. This is not good." At the center of the chaos was Xavian. Actually, to be perfectly clear, the chaos was Xavian.

His pants were down, and he was pooping—in the middle of the large dog park. I was in shock. By that point, I was sprinting to him. I didn't know what I would do once I reached him, but I sprinted nonetheless. Once I reached him, he was pulling his pants back up. I asked him why he just pooped in the dog park. His reasoning? He said there were two reasons: one, there was no restroom nearby; and two, big boys aren't supposed to poop in their pants. His logic was actually quite sound. The only problem was we didn't have toilet paper at the dog park, since dogs don't use toilet paper.

At that point, amid my embarrassment and frustration over what had just happened, there was only one thing to do—show him grace and show him love. This was a teaching moment, and the lesson was grace. To add, by then I had gotten to the point where I didn't care what other people thought, so if anyone at the dog park had an issue with what they had just witnessed, they were best suited to keep it to themselves. Luckily, no one said a word, but we definitely got some stares from a few others that day. They were humorously bewildered. As much as I want to respect and love people, I admit that my proverbial guns were loaded to defend Xavian and our situation, just in case. Most of all, my heart broke for Xavian, a nine-year-old boy who didn't understand that he shouldn't go poop in front of people in a dog park.

When Cassie arrived, she saw the petrified look on my face and immediately knew something was amiss. There was no proof of what had happened, as I had used a doggy bag to pick it up, but as I explained the situation to Cassie, I got exactly what I expected from her—*uncontrollable laughter*.

In the grand scheme of things, it simply wasn't a big issue. He had to go, so he went, then we cleaned it up and life continued. As tough of a moment as that was for me, cold, muddy, and perplexed, I was proud of myself for giving Xavian the only two things he needed at the time—love and grace. It also makes for a great story.

I hope this, as well as the rest of Xavian's story, has painted a picture of how abundant grace truly is.

HOPE, FAITH, AND GRATITUDE

As we continue to move forward in time, sensing but not truly knowing what's ahead of us, my mind goes to a few unseen places.

Have you ever felt so incredibly helpless that you believed you weren't adequate enough to take care of one of your children? I have. In fact, because of my feelings of inadequacy with Xavian, I've explored those feelings which lie buried in the deepest recesses of my heart. I'm sure many parents who have children with special needs have felt the same. Reality forces us to dig deep, whether we naturally work that way or not. When the struggle remains constant, it's normal to begin doubting yourself. It's easy to fall victim to the blinders that suggest you aren't doing amazing things during times of heightened stress.

Don't misunderstand me. I'm not accepting the feeling

that I am an inadequate parent as truth, rather I've looked deeply into the reasons that such a notion would enter my mind in the first place. It's a painful, gut-wrenching, debilitating thing to think about.

On the other end of this rabbit hole of feared inadequacy lies the false fantasy of what it would be like to be free of the responsibility and self-doubt, to have a life without a child with special needs. One might imagine it to be a world of comfort, one where we go wherever we want, whenever we want, without fear of all of the things which we currently face in our reality. I just can't imagine such a perfect reality exists, so I back out of that rabbit hole as quickly as I possibly can, every single time.

Hope is a state of optimism. It is also a gift. Hope is not part of a religion or a sexual designation, although hope is often used as a core value in such things. Hope is much bigger than that. Anyone can have hope. People can place their hope in whatever they feel, and that can be different for every person. One person's hope in a certain thing does not diminish or invalidate another person's in a totally different thing, even if those things oppose one another or one person claims truth in theirs. We are here together, breathing, mysteriously existing, wanting answers, but not always getting the answers we desire.

That's where faith comes in. Faith, in my opinion, is when

someone is presented with options, none of the options fully add up or give the person a clear, doubtless truth, so the person makes a choice in what they will believe. This is faith. Faith creates a strong desire in someone to believe in something. Faith can lead to hope, but they aren't the same thing. Faith is a belief. Hope is an attitude. My heart breaks a hundred times a day for my son and others like him, and each time, driven by *hope* and held up by *faith*, it comes back a hundred times stronger. People don't get through journeys such as ours without hope and faith. They are immense difference makers and the necessary foundations on which we stand.

I wrote this book because I felt like our story needed to be told from a father's perspective. In circumstances similar to ours, or really in family life in general, fathers can easily get lost in the shuffle. So often, we aren't masculine enough in the eyes of people or society and we're told we need to "toughen up," while other times, we aren't feminine enough for them, so we need to "be more sensitive." This leads to a constant emotional tug-of-war to please others, and neurotic guilt when we can't achieve perfection.

I wrote about feeling invisible at times throughout our journey. These feelings aren't isolated to me or my situation. Other fathers struggle with the same types of things. I want fathers to know they can be leaders if they want. They can also stand side-by-side with their wife, or even behind their wife if she needs to lead in a given situation. Single and married fathers can show their children the same feminine love and affection that mothers are traditionally better known for providing.

Find what works best for you and your family and go with that. Don't let Society tell you how to run your family. Dive deeply into your household dynamic and work it out. Times have changed. Women are doing a lot more than they could sixty years ago, which opens the door for men to do different things than they did sixty years ago. It all shifts around like air. I encourage men to embrace that. Support your family in whatever ways they need to be supported, without being bound to outdated ideals and without being told, "Fathers don't do that."

Fathers, you are not some Neanderthal cave man whose sole purpose is to go out and bash a poor, unsuspecting animal over the head with a club. You're a modern man and there are millions of people who endorse you as a sensitive, gentle, loving being who can clean your home or fold clothes, or play dolls with your child. Be the strong, courageous soul who is ready to fight to the death for his family, but don't lose sight of the fact that you are so much more. Be everything to your family, while at the absolute very least being a decent person to the rest of the world.

I wrote about tears because I wanted fathers to understand the healing effect tears offer. Crying is an ability you possess and should use. If you're too embarrassed to cry in front of people, I get that. Do it in private. When I'm able to cry, it's almost always in private. I've found it nearly impossible to cry in front of my family. I'm not sure why that's the case, but it doesn't matter. You have to roll with what works, so that's what I do.

I also needed to write this book for myself, as part of a long, slow, painful healing process brought on by the trauma which I acquired from fighting the very battle I've written about in this book. I knew this was coming before I realized it was actually going to happen. Call it a gut feeling. By 2019, in addition to the trauma I was already sifting through, I was in the latter stages of deep spiritual and emotional pain as a result of loss and rejection. I prayed for quite some time for God to help me understand the purpose of the pain from that situation because I was struggling to see clearly. I guess I felt like something that had affected me so deeply couldn't be for nothing—and I was right.

Because so many pathways had been opened in my soul, I was able to reach feelings and words I otherwise couldn't, so I began writing regularly. I primarily wrote poetry because telling stories metaphorically came natural to me, as did making words rhyme. These stories organically flowed out of my heart in a poetic manner. Writing felt natural, and while poetry allowed me to hone in on my creativity, I needed to build something from the ground up, something more complex. I needed bigger projects. That's when I heard God say, "Write this book." At first I laughed it off, but after a few days of feeling God stare at me awkwardly, I heard it again, "Write this book."

Indifferent to the idea of writing a book, I smirked and said, "I guess I'm going to write this book." Then I started writing, and experiencing healing like you would not believe. One perpetually bloody war, one perplexingly painful situation, and one novel-length memoir later, and I am full of gratitude for all the growth and soul repair I've worked through.

Finally, I needed to write this book to send a message of purpose. Far too often, purpose isn't considered in the journey of life. It's treated like nothing, when in fact it's everything. It's absolutely everything. If you are fighting, or have fought, one of life's bloody mental, emotional, spiritual, or physical wars and you are in pain, please understand there is immense purpose in that pain. Sometimes you have to wait until the smoke clears to find that purpose. It usually takes time, which results in discomfort, but that discomfort is what allows us to access parts of ourselves we otherwise cannot reach. It is in these places where purpose can be accessed, examined, and understood. Purpose is always there, waiting for you to find it, and that purpose is always a gift.

What resonates with me the most from our journey is *grat-*

itude. While faith gives strength, hope produces perseverance, and purpose offers motivation, gratitude churns out a never-ending supply of humility. Gratitude crushes resentment and replaces it with a humble spirit. Like hope, gratitude is an attitude, and I feel like what often gets overlooked is that gratitude is an important ingredient in hope. When it seems all is lost and there is no tomorrow, there is always something to be grateful for.

It took me a long time to get to a point where I could remind myself every day how grateful I should be for, at the very least, *life*. If everything else is stripped away, you've searched your heart and found nothing to be grateful for—remember that life always remains, and that is enough. Gratitude gives us the motivation, organically, that we need to rise up when those frustrating and difficult moments have us pinned to the ground, telling us that there is no tomorrow and that we have already lost the battle. The truth is, the battle isn't over because we're still breathing.

Gratitude doesn't require us to have a smile on our faces, and it doesn't need us to ignore the reality of our situation. It just needs us to know that there are gifts, and all we have to do is acknowledge those gifts as something special and something bigger than us. An attitude of gratitude doesn't mean we aren't stressed, struggling, concerned, unsure, sad, or depressed. It means we're able to clearly see and accept all that we have, even in those difficult emotional states. Being thankful easily gets buried when people are hurting. From an atmospheric perspective, it's human nature.

Gratitude yearns to be found, but it requires a certain level of deliberation. This intentional act of deliberation, in and of itself, usually proves to be therapeutic for people during difficult times. Having gratitude is crying uncontrollably from the exhaustion of caring for a child with special needs, but instead of asking for it all to go away, thanking God for those precious moments of respite, those rare victories, and the joy in our hearts that still remains somehow. Being the father of a child with cancer and special needs is not the life I could have ever imagined, and certainly not one I would have chosen had I been given the opportunity to pick from a candy jar full of lives. It is, however, the life I'm infinitely grateful for, and that makes all the difference in the world.

There will be hardships, struggles, and disappointment. Life is designed that way. I want people to know it's okay. Not to sound too morbid, but we will all pass from this place at some point in time. At the end of our lives, we'll all look back and realize how interminable the journey seemed, but in reality how transient it truly was. It will serve us well to look beyond the pain and discomfort which unapologetically created barriers, challenges, and anxiety in our individual quests.

My desire is that our story will provide hope to anyone

battling anything that seems insurmountable. Our story isn't limited to inspiring parents of cancer survivors or parents of children with special needs, rather it's for anyone, anywhere, going through *anything*. Not everyone will place their faith in what we placed our faith in. That is understandable and I accept it fully, but everyone can have an optimistic attitude about what is to come—an attitude of hope—an attitude of gratitude. This freedom is available for everyone, there for the taking.

To this day, whenever I drive down Interstate 65 in Birmingham, Alabama, and I see that rangy, reflective, regal tower better known as Children's Hospital of Alabama, rising high above the surrounding buildings, I'm plunged into a wide range of emotions that, if mixed properly, form the perfect tears:

A touch of empathy.

A hint of remorse.

A sliver of gratitude.

A dab of regret.

A drop of love.

And a pinch of pain.

If my heart is vulnerable enough at the time, the tears flow, with each emotion shimmering, glistening, and reminding me that the old cliche is perhaps more profound than we realize—while the days are awfully long and the years are terribly short, we are capable of incomprehensible feats. And God is supernaturally loyal in that.

I'm prepared for my son's eventuality, which is no different than any of ours—death. In reality, one version of him left us when he was a baby. In my oft-visited future-thinking mind, he's left us many times, and I've felt that loss each time. I don't think I'll ever escape the trauma brought on by the heartache I've felt during this journey, but I don't think I have to. It's not always about getting *past* things, as sometimes it's more about adjusting and learning to live *with* things. For me, adjusting and fighting through this has carried a tremendous amount of purpose, the purpose of finding gratitude, and the purpose of striving to be a better father. The journey has been fruitful, and I am grateful for the suffering and purpose that is yet to come.

THE HILLSIDE

*T*here was just me, all alone in a foreign land which somehow felt so familiar. This place couldn't be found on a map or seen from outer space. It wasn't here or there or anywhere really. It just existed—somewhere.

A four-hundred-year-old Angel Oak tree highlighted the horizon where it stood majestically, anchored high above the forest's edge, overlooking a beautiful countryside where a small European-like town sat nestled amongst a series of grassy, rolling hills. As the sun shone down through the tree's leaves, their shadows appeared, disappeared, and reappeared against the tall gold grass in a glorious, choreographed dance.

Feelings of gratitude coursed through my veins in hair-raising fashion as I sat alone near the base of the glorious Angel Oak, deep in thought, contemplating what was, what is, but mostly what would come to be. *This was my fortress of solitude as I considered difficult matters. A strong breeze steadily flurried through, over fields of gold, in waves of harmony. I thought surely the grassy fields would tire, but they seemed to gain energy as the day grew long. Likewise, a shallow stream tiptoed its way back and forth down the mountain, into the forest, and eventually into the town below. Light glistened as the water rippled over every rock.*

If the shadows provided the dance, and the wind the harmony, then the stream delivered the melody. The mild air was captivating. I felt safe in that place, like a bear cub with its mom. I leaned back against a mossy rock which rested like a baby near the base of the great tree. Everything felt—balanced. Beyond the surrounding mountains were taller mountains, towering in the distance. Further beyond the tall mountains stood colossal ones, their apexes disappearing into the heavens. Not even the clouds could contain them. It was all so surreal.

There was nowhere to go, nothing to do. I sat motionless as time lent itself to me so that I could ponder every inch of my soul, my spirit, the universe, and God. As resentment, grief, sorrow, and all the negative emotions sought to overtake me, the feelings of gratitude rushed forward to empower me and reign supreme. And it came to pass, after all the highs and lows, the excitement and pain, I finally rested. Like a wounded warrior who was home after a wayward war, I rested. The last remaining light reached subtly into my emotions, while tears transformed into butterflies and fluttered away with the wind. Shadows grew so long that neither their beginning or end could be found. Eventually, I became one with the shadows, absent like the light. I was home. No more blood. No more death. Only life. The journey was over.

ACKNOWLEDGEMENTS

Thanks so much Kayli Baker for your beta reading and copy-editing magic that helped turn my grey caterpillar manuscript into a beautiful butterfly book. I can't imagine this coming together without you. I'm so proud to call you my friend. No one will ever believe how we met.

A special thanks to Kym Mitchell and Sasha Ramini for the extraordinary way in which you have touched our souls. You'll never know how truly thankful we are for you both.

To all of our family and friends who moved our home for us, brought us food during hospital stays, drove across state lines to help us, prayed for us, and offered to stay at the hospital with Xavian, or keep Dante and Larkin, thank you. You're amazing.

For The Cheesemans from Wisconsin, we were neighbors for a short time, but you took Dante in and loved him like he was your own child while we struggled to make sense of things. We'll never forget you.

We're indescribably grateful for all of Xavian's teachers and paraprofessionals who put themselves in harm's way on a daily basis and allowed verbal and physical assaults to roll off their shoulders like rain drops down a window. Thank you so much.

Thanks to Denise and Vonda, our moms, for being there when we've needed you, and Barry and Tom, our fathers, for your encouragement along the way.

Without a dedicated team of medical professionals who were committed to providing the best care possible for Xavian, as well as the most logical path forward for our family, we would have been lost. We're thankful for each of you.

Smile-A-Mile, aTeam Ministries, Haven, Ady's Army, Magic Moments, Blue Skies Ministries, and Project Angel Hugs, the selfless work you do has impacted us throughout our journey, and we'll never forget how much your love has given us the lift we've needed.

And to you, the reader, thanks so much for reading my book. I hope our story has impacted you in a positive way.

NOTE FROM THE AUTHOR

Writing this book cost me time, pain, and plenty of tears. It was also cathartic and life-changing, and helped me become a better father. The story of The Other Boy is told from a father's perspective, so I hope it can help not only fathers, but anyone who has experienced unexpected life struggles and trauma. I want readers to feel the things we went through during our journey, as the pressure steadily mounted for more than a decade. I want readers to see that in my suffering I explored the deeply emotional side of what could have been in order to better appreciate and accept what actually was, by using one of my most powerful gifts—imagination. Ultimately, I want readers to understand that it's okay to be in pain and to struggle, and that during their battles they can choose an attitude of hope and find hidden treasures therein, including one of the most elusive but precious treasures of all—*gratitude*.

ABOUT THE AUTHOR

M. Stephens Hall developed a deep imagination at a very young age. He often visited fantastic worlds where he unearthed profound possibilities. Although he didn't write early in life, he found plenty of creative outlets through which to express himself. He later received his Bachelor of Science degree in Computer Science from Mississippi College, and has spent over twenty years using his creativity and problem-solving skills in software development. As his intuition matured, M. Stephens began writing more frequently and with more purpose, often early in the morning before work. Poetry served him a healing mechanism during difficult times and offered a gateway into writing books. M. Stephens enjoys providing and caring for his family, exercising, adventuring, and of course, writing.

mstephenshall.com

REFERENCES

Temple of the Dog, Chris Cornell, and Eddie Vedder. "Say Hello to Heaven." Temple of the Dog, A&M Records, 1991.

Collier, Lorna. "Why We Cry." American Psychological Association, 2014, Vol 45, No. 2, apa.org.

Garbes, Angela. "The More I Learn About Breast Milk, the More Amazed I Am." The Stranger, 2015, thestranger.com.

"The Chicken Roaster." Seinfeld, created by Larry David and Jerry Seinfeld. Season 8, Episode 8, NBC, 1996.

"11 Facts About Hurricane Katrina." DoSomething.org, dosomething.org.

"Jim & Andy: The Great Beyond." Directed by Chris Smith. Starring Jim Carrey. VICE Films, Netflix, 2017.

"The Matrix." Directed by Lana Wachowski and Lilly Wachowski. Starring Keanu Reeves, Laurence Fishburne, and Carrie-Anne

Moss. Warner Bros, 1999.

"The Terminator." Directed by James Cameron. Starring Arnold Schwarzenegger. Orion Pictures, 1984.

"Back to the Future." Directed by Robert Zemeckis. Starring Michael J. Fox and Christopher Lloyd. Universal Pictures, 1985.

"The Last Dance." Directed by Jason Hehir. Episode IX, ESPN Films, April 19, 2020.

Eddie Vedder. "Society." Into the Wild, J Records, 2007.

Schwarz, John H. "String Theory." Symmetry, 2007, symmetry-magazine.org.

BEC Crew, "Scientists Propose a 'Mirror Universe' Where Time Moves Backwards." Science Alert, 2016, sciencealert.com.

Brown, Brené. "Listening to Shame." TED, 2012, ted.com.

"The Croods." Directed by Kirk DeMicco and Chris Sanders. DreamWorks Animation, 2013.

9 781736 638804